Diana, thank you for the op[*a remarkable journey of resilie1* *wishes in getting the book publis*

Rea Former Legal Counsel to the ....
International Law Professor, U.S. Naval War College
Professional Lecturer, GW University Elliott School of International Law

You will find yourself hungry for the kind of deep God-intimacy you have experienced as you have devoured the pages of this book. You won't want it to end — you will return to read it again (just like I have) — and you will want to share it with friends. Victory in The Valley — *through the words of your new-found friend, Diana — will be one of those rare books you will treasure always for the boundless hope — encouragement — and strength it provides.*

Lovingly read — reread — and treasured by **Pam Wolf**
Entrepreneur, Speaker, Business Success Coach
Founder of Identity and Destiny / Christian Women of Influence
Co-Author of "Finding Your God Given Sweet Spot"

I am sure that this book will become a soft pillow for the hearts of folks who read it. Thanks for being obedient in the writing.

Dale Schlafer, Co-founder & President
Center for World Revival & Awakening
Chairman of the Board, Promise Keepers (Inception to 1994)
Senior Pastor, South Fellowship Church, Littleton, CO (22 years)

With open-hearted vulnerability, Diana Furr invites us into her life. Through her wonder-filled stories, we can learn secrets that allow us all to be victorious overcomers. This book testifies to the living power of Jesus of Nazareth in the life of someone who is totally dependent upon and in love with Him. Read on, it will be time well spent as you will be blessed.

Priscilla Flory

Diana Furr's ability to be authentic and transparent about her successes and struggles, but at the same time, keep her eye on the eternal purposes of God, is truly awe-inspiring. She proves that we can always trust God, even when we can't always track His footsteps. I will be referring to and recommending her book to any person I know who desperately needs to find purpose in their pain, security in their suffering, or a testimony in their trials. This book is a must-read.

Dr. Joe Martin, Founder of RealMenConnect.com
Host of The Real Men Connect Podcast,
#1-Rated Podcast on iTunes for Christian Men

An old song says there's a lonesome valley we all must walk . . . by ourselves. Without faith, these words are true; with faith, they need not be, for if we know the Lord, we never have to walk that vale alone.

The valley in question is known by several names in Scripture: "The valley of the shadow of death," and "The valley of Baka" (the valley of weeping) are two of them. Some pilgrims never find their way out; some pretend they never were there. But there is a better way; specifically, by practicing the seven secrets Diana learned through her journey into and out of a valley named cancer.

This valley has other names, too — as many names as there are causes of a broken heart. And the reason this book will help anyone in distress is because Diana has embraced the calling of 2 Corinthians 1:3-5: "Praise be to the God and Father of our Lord Jesus Christ, the Father of compassion and the God of all comfort, who comforts us in all our troubles, so that we can comfort those in any trouble with the comfort we ourselves receive from God."

As an editor and publisher, I read perhaps 3 million words a year. Many of them are just squiggles of black against a backdrop of white. But the words of this book are "like apples of gold in settings of silver" (Proverbs 25:11). You will treasure and keep them, but you'll also want to share them with friends.

David B. Biebel, DMin, Minister, Author, Editor, Publisher
Author of CBA Gold Medallion Award-winner, "New Light on Depression"
and bestseller, "If God Is So Good, Why Do I Hurt So Bad?"

Victory
in
The Valley

*7 Secrets to Overcoming Life's Worst
and Savoring Life's Best*

DIANA S. FURR

Published by:

Healthy Life Press • Denver, CO 80219
www.healthylifepress.com

Author: Diana S. Furr, AfC, MBA
Designer: Judy Johnson

Printed in the United States of America

Library of Congress Cataloging-in-Publication Data
Furr, Diana S.
Victory in The Valley

ISBN 978-1-939267-03-0
1. Biography & Autobiography / Religious 2. Religion / Christian Life / Personal Growth

Unless otherwise identified, Scripture quotations are taken from The Holy Bible, New International Version®, NIV®. Copyright © 1973, 1978, 1984, 2011 by Biblica, Inc.® Used by permission.

Capitalizations that do not conform to the *Zondervan Christian Writer's Manual of Style* are the author's choice, for emphasis.

Disclaimer: The opinions expressed in this book are those of the author, and may or may not represent the official views of Healthy Life Press, its Publisher, or any of its other authors.

Most Healthy life Press resources are available wherever books are sold. Distribution is primarily through *Amazon.com, deepershopping.com*, and *healthylifepress.com*. Multiple copy discounts available directly from Healthy Life Press. Wholesale distribution is through *springarbor.com* (a division of *IngramContent.com*), and *deepershopping.com*. Our ePublications are available through *healthylifepress.com, Amazon.com* (Kindle), *BN.com* (Nook), and for all eBook readers through *deepershopping.com*. Wholesale pricing is available through *IngramContent.com* (*springarbor.com*).

Contents

This is for You, Lord . . .
with Forever Love and Gratitude.

For turning my "nothings" into "somethings."
And making my "somethings" . . . Priceless.

Come away with Me
to My Secret Place.

You will tell me the desires of your heart
. . . and I will tell you Mine.

Then, you will go out from Me
. . . and tell people about Me.

And many, many people
will be greatly, greatly blessed.

A Prophecy
1995

Introduction

I didn't believe in Miracles.
For more than half of my life.

Now, it seems, I see one around almost every corner . . .
almost every day.

And I can't stop talking about them. I also call them "God Stories."
People who know me have come to expect to hear one or two of these
stories in almost every conversation we share.

What is a Miracle anyway? Oxford Dictionaries online defines it as
*"an extraordinary and welcome event that is not explicable by natural or
scientific laws and is therefore attributed to a divine agency."*

Maybe that's why I didn't believe in Miracles.
Because I didn't believe in "a divine agency."

I believe *now*.
And He isn't just some "divine agency."
He's my dearest Friend.

Maybe that's why there's nothing I love more than telling people about the Miracles of Walking through Life with Jesus. Wherever He may lead.

I have written to Him — *about* Him — almost every day for the last five years. *Thousands* of pages, documenting *thousands* of my encounters with Him.

Encounters — and the "Secrets" they embody — that have *blessed* me and *changed* me forever.

But which should I share here? Which should I leave out? How do I pull them together in a way that, hopefully, will bless <u>others</u> as He has blessed <u>me</u>?

I was overwhelmed just thinking about it.

Maybe that's why this assignment from Him — the writing of this book — has been on the "back burner" for five years. Maybe it's just that its time has finally come.

I started out with thirteen "Secrets."

Why *thirteen*?

Some call it a "Baker's Dozen." Some think it's a harbinger of bad luck. For me, the number thirteen has always been an expression of God's *Amazing Grace*. His *Miraculous* Grace. His *Impossible* Grace.

A number that is special to *me* . . . because *He* chose to make that number special for *Us*.

The "Us" that is . . .

. . . a loving Father and His once-wounded, still-healing Daughter.

. . . a passionate Savior and His once-soiled, still-imperfect Bride.

. . . a patient Holy Spirit and His once-clueless, still-learning Student.

. . . a King of kings and His once-defiant, still-surrendering Leader.

Why thirteen? Because . . .

. . . thirteen years passed between the Greatest Evil ever committed against me and the Greatest Evil I ever committed in response. And . . .

. . . another thirteen years passed between my Greatest Evil and my Adoption into the Family of the God who gave His Life so I could *begin to truly* Live . . . now and forever.

But I get ahead of myself.

Victory in The Valley is woven around my latest trek . . . through the Valley of the Shadow of Breast Cancer. The Valley *into* which the Lord I love led me. The Valley *in* which the Lord I love *taught* me. The Valley *through* which the Lord I love *carried* me.

The Valley where the Lord I love *encountered* me . . . in ways that have forever changed the way I *live* and *lead*. I hope what He has led me to share here will do the same for you.

A funny thing happened to me as I traveled through this Valley of the Shadow. I didn't know what The Future might hold . . . or if I would even *have* a future. So, I started having Flashbacks. To Valleys of other kinds, and Victories (or failures) from earlier times.

I was not surprised that many Flashbacks came from my lifelong business career. The Lord made me into a leader long before I knew Him. I started work when I was fourteen years old. One thing led to another, and I found myself earning degrees and accomplishing business results in leadership roles that far surpassed anything I had ever imagined.

But my PhD in the "School of Hard Knocks" began earlier. Much earlier. Some of that "schooling" comes through in this book, too.

That's how my journey through the Valley of the Shadow took shape. "Flashbacks" to former days, where memories and past insights had relevance for my present needs. "Fast Forwards" to my battle with cancer, where unique experiences added new dimensions to even my past understandings. So, that's the "rhythm" of this book — Flashbacks and Fast Forwards.

Maybe it's impossible to confront our own mortality and *not* reflect on all that came before. Maybe it's inevitable for the Giver of Life to remind us of His All-Sufficient Grace in every *past* valley — to empower us to reach for Him in the *current* one.

My "every *past* valley" filled thousands of pages with hundreds of Secrets. I started this book with thirteen. I ended up with seven. Because sometimes, quite simply, Less is More. Is this how John felt when he was sorting through what *he* would tell the world about Jesus?

> *"Jesus did many other things as well.*
> *If every one of them were written down,*
> *I suppose that even the whole world*
> *would not have enough room*
> *for the books that would be written."*
> (John 21:25)

Maybe there's another book in my future. Maybe not. But I hope *this* one does whatever *He* wants it to do in the hearts of those *He* prompts to read it. Will you be one of them?

Thankfully, we won't *all* have breast cancer; only one woman in eight. ["Only"??? That's *a lot* of women!] But we *all* have Valleys — in Life and in Leadership. And these 7 Secrets — and the Victory they promise — are relevant in any and every Valley we may ever encounter.

Victory in The Valley is drawn largely from my journal notes — my ongoing conversation with my Lord. My circumstances, questions, petitions and praises. And His answers — both tangible and intangible.

I invite you to eavesdrop on our relationship, in the Hope that you may be encouraged and empowered, as I have been . . .

. . . to find Victory in *your* Valley —
even if you are still in the middle of it.

*"Now to Him who is able to do
immeasurably more than all we ask or imagine,
according to His power that is at work within us,
to Him be glory in the church and in Christ Jesus
throughout all generations, for ever and ever! Amen."*
(Ephesians 3:20)

Secret #1

Admit the Obvious: You're Not in Control.
So, turn to the Only One who is.

Even Cancer needs a Context.

Flashback . . .

I had just retired from my latest Leadership Adventure. One of those *unprecedented* and *unparalleled* invitations that You, Lord, extend with equal measures of delight and anticipation.

My Adventure at Samaritan's Touch Care Center lasted seven years. A vibrant, Christian primary and specialized health care center that You, Lord, *miraculously* raised up out of *nothing*. In the second poorest county in Florida. A medical and spiritual outreach to uninsured, financially-struggling patients. The "Working Poor."

By Your grace, I was in on the ground floor. When "The Miracle-to-Come" was still just an idea. A 20-year-old, dormant idea . . . *whose time had arrived*. Suddenly, You began to move and we were running as fast as we could to keep up!

At Your choosing, Lord, I became Your spark. The leader You would use to ignite our whole community with a sense of Awe and Expectancy.

Always looking UP.

The spark became a wildfire as I "testified" before businesses, health care providers, elected officials, churches, service organizations, and many others. Sharing stories of *Miracles*. Miracles whose Source became, over time, both unmistakable and irresistible.

"Look what the Lord is doing! Look what the Lord is doing!"

People *did* look. And they *saw*.
And people of <u>every</u> faith — and <u>no</u> faith —
wanted to join You!

The scope of the health care You were mobilizing, Lord — on behalf of "the least" in our community — seemed to have no limits. Even "smoking embers" in the most reticent hearts were stoked into flames of Generosity.

Before we even had an organization, a donor stepped forward with an in-kind donation of land, buildings and equipment estimated to be worth $500,000. Funding was mobilized to support a core, full-time medical staff, prescription medications, plus other operating expenses.

Strategic partnerships with key providers yielded comprehensive lab work and other sophisticated diagnostics like X-rays, CT-scans and MRIs. Some 170 medical volunteers agreed to donate their expertise in a myriad of specialties that went well beyond basic primary care — including surgeries of various kinds, as well as *comprehensive* eye, dental and cancer care.

And it was all donated!

What happened was even *bigger* than the Vision You had *dared* us to believe at the beginning of our journey with You, Lord. Samaritan's Touch would not be just an informal, neighborhood clinic operating one evening a week. It would become a sophisticated medical facility open *full-time*, providing comprehensive health care services Mondays through Fridays.

But *before* all that came to be, we were just a little project team. Heading into a vast ocean of uncharted waters. Traveling in what seemed to be a little rowboat. And I will never forget the moment You asked me to take the "helm."

In the natural, I would never have been hired to found and lead a medical facility such as this. I had no medical credentials, no medical training, no health care managerial experience of any kind.

I told You as much . . . the day You "tapped" me on the shoulder. I could almost feel Your Touch . . . and there was no doubting Your Intention. You were inviting me to become the first Executive Director at Samaritan's Touch.

"But, Lord," I said,
"my only experience in health care is as a patient."

Your answer was simple and to the point:
"Get out of the boat . . . and follow Me."

You already knew what You were about to do. You just wanted us to be willing to take a small step — no, *a giant leap* — of Faith.

So, I did. Others followed.

And You proceeded to "bless our socks off"
. . . with Miracles too numerous to count! ☺

The fullness of this story — *Your Story, Lord* — remains to be told another day. But at last count, by Your abundant mercy, Samaritan's Touch has delivered over $36 million in donated, high-quality medical care to over 2,700 patients, through over 67,000 patient visits . . . blessing thousands all the way to Eternity.

You exceeded our highest — *and wildest* — expectations, Lord! And from a leadership perspective, isn't that the very result **Secret #1** is designed to produce?

Admit the Obvious: You're Not in Control.
So, turn to the Only One who is.

By helping us move beyond the limits of our proven experience . . . and *boldly* go where we have never been before???

Fast Forward . . .

Why would any leader "worth her salt" retire early, Lord — at age 59 — from a Labor of Love so intense? Or from the opportunity to leave such a practical and powerful Legacy of Your Love? Only for *another* Labor of Love — <u>also</u> intense, in a different way?

How about a once-in-a-lifetime, extended cross-country adventure with my dear husband? From the orange groves of Florida to the wilderness of Alaska. In a travel trailer, no less?!

<u>Another</u> 20-year-old, dormant idea *whose time had arrived*. But a six-month vacation? For two committed (driven?) career professionals who rarely managed the "luxury" of even *one* week off per year?

A new Adventure, indeed!

Knowing the "why" is one thing. But the "how" is easier said than done. How does the brain wrap itself around a totally new lifestyle? And how does the heart then catch up with the brain?

> *"Lord, please peel my fingers away from*
> *this precious work I have loved so much.*
> *This work You have called me to do.*
> *So I can support my husband's dream fully, with a pure heart.*
> *So I can hold my life in an open hand, and <u>gladly</u> let <u>You</u> have <u>Your</u> way."*

It took one year for Your answer to fully come, Lord. But come, it did. I retired from Samaritan's Touch on January 31 that year. Two weeks later, we bought our travel trailer and set our target departure date.

Two weeks after that, my world turned upside down.

I was lying in bed at 10:30 PM, reading (as I often did) before going to sleep. My husband was snoozing next to me. And a Voice that was almost audible — *Your* Voice, Lord — spoke to me:

"Check your left breast."

Hmm . . . You had never said anything quite like that to me before. So I reached down . . . and put my hand on a huge tumor.

My mind shot out thoughts like a semi-automatic. How could this be? I had yearly physicals and mammograms and frequent breast self-exams . . . always normal. For this tumor to have grown so large since my last self-check, it must be *aggressive*. And the aggressive "stuff" is usually not benign . . .

The next morning, I scheduled a diagnostic mammogram and ultrasound . . . and stepped fully into **Secret #1**:

Admit the Obvious: You're Not in Control.
So turn to the Only One who is.

How would You describe my first prayer, Lord? It was not a Desperate Wailing. It was more of a Declaration of Willingness. Speaking truths from my heart-of-hearts to You, Lord — *The* Heart of my heart:

You <u>know</u> I will ask You for healing, Lord —
even <u>miraculous</u> healing, if that is what it takes.
And I will ask in complete <u>faith</u>, knowing You are ABLE . . .
IF that is what You choose to do.

I also know You are Sovereign.
And if this <u>does</u> turn out to be cancer,
I know You will have allowed it into my life . . .
for Your <u>good</u> <u>purposes</u>.

You also know <u>my</u> heart, Lord, is that
my life would count as much as possible for You

for however long You leave me on the planet.

So if You, in Your Sovereignty, say
my life can count more for You
with me having cancer than without it,
I'm OK with that.

"OK" doesn't mean I will like everything I go through.
"OK" doesn't mean I will always respond
in a godly way to everything I go through.

But being "OK" with it is truly my heart.
And I <u>know</u> You will give me everything I need
as we travel through this Valley together.

So, have Your way, Lord . . .
and 'milk it' for all it's worth to You, for eternity's sake!

The wilderness of Alaska was already off my radar screen. Because somehow I *knew* . . . a Wilderness of a *different* kind was now looming ahead.

My new full-time "career" had become Trip Preparation — assembling the gear we would need for our journey to Alaska. If the Wilderness had now shifted, I would need vastly different "gear." So as I awaited my diagnostics, I assembled *that* gear as best I could.

February 21: O Lord, have mercy.
Dearest Lord, do not let Your enemies gain the victory.
Put a hedge of protection around us. Give us favor, Lord.
Encourage our hearts. Show Yourself mighty, Beloved.

February 23: O Lord, how awesome!
You know the desires of my heart.
They are Your desires far more than mine!
Beloved, Your mercies are new this morning.
I enter into this day with great thanksgiving.
I give myself to The Potter's hand.

February 24: *Maybe the best part of the day*
(after my time with You, Lord)
was telling my husband about the tumor
and the diagnostics I have scheduled.
It was the right thing to do.
I didn't want him to worry if it was a false alarm.
But we are "in it" — Life, with all its twists and turns — together.
Thank You, Lord, for the gift of a life partner who is so dear.

February 25: *"Some trust in chariots and some in horses,*
but we trust in the name of the Lord our God." (Psalm 20:7).
So do not fear, Diana — God is with you.
Nothing can overcome the mighty strength of the Lord.
Trust Him for your victory.
Thank You, Lord!
The battle and the Victory are <u>Yours</u>!!!

Of course, we're never just bystanders on the sidelines . . . are we, Lord? We still must *show* up, *suit* up and *arm* up for every battle. Maybe that's why I have come to love **Secret #1**:

Admit the Obvious: You're Not in Control.
So turn to the Only One who is.

Because through **Secret #1**, You not only help us learn *how* to show up, suit up, and arm up. You also help us have *Hope* and *Faith* to persevere through whatever is yet to come.

And here's the thing: *Every* promise about Your Victory is true, Lord. Yet sometimes, You don't take us *out* of the Valley to *prove* it . . . do You?

You lead us *into* the Valley . . .
where Your Victory is all the sweeter.

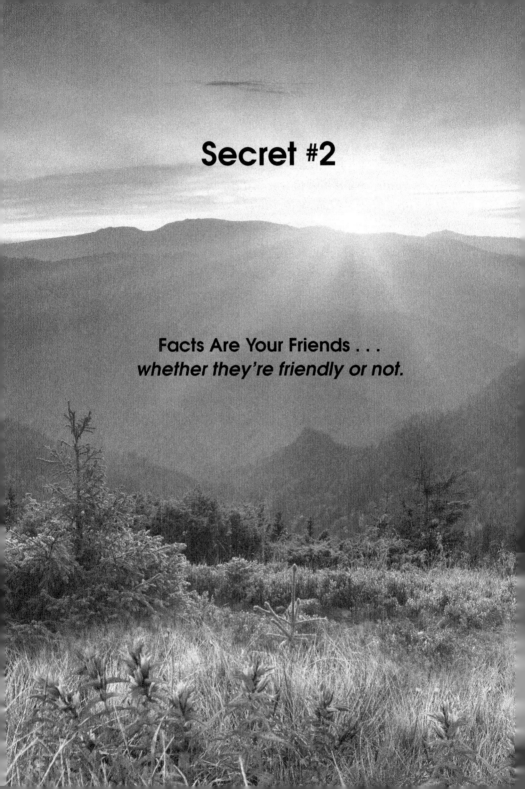

Secret #2

Facts Are Your Friends . . .
whether they're friendly or not.

Flashback...

As a leader, I have always ascribed to the wisdom that "Information is Power."

Not the power to "lord over" others. For me, leadership has always been about igniting journeys of self-discovery in the people I have been privileged to influence. Helping them release their untapped potential and then engage more effectively with others. So that, *together,* we can all accomplish much greater outcomes than what is possible when we work apart.

You were instilling this leadership style in me long before I met You... weren't You, Lord? Little by little. Long before I could discern Your Presence or credit Your Grace. Long before I fell (and grew) in love with You.

Like when I became "The Chicken Lady" at McCormick & Company — the #1 spice company in the world. I hadn't set out to earn that nickname. I just did some things that, at the time, seemed to move right past "creative" all the way to "crazy." ☺

I had been given the privilege of helping to develop and launch a new line of products. They were geared to capitalize on increasingly healthy eating trends. Less red meat. More chicken and fish.

"Chicken Sauce Blends" began as five "gourmet" meals formulated for boneless chicken breasts. Five foil pouches — each one filled with all the herbs and spices needed for busy cooks to create a scrumptious meal in 20 minutes. Just add the chicken and the prescribed liquid.

Shortly before our national launch, the cost of raw materials and packaging skyrocketed . . . wiping out our projected first-year net profit. We couldn't change the goal, so how could we change the outcome? I knew the manufacturing process would be key. If only the line workers could become even more efficient and effective . . .

But I had seen the machinery in action. Foil packages flew by so quickly, they were a blur to the human eye. How could we help those workers develop a *personal relationship* with these five new products? So they had a vested interest in their success?

I went to my friend in the manufacturing plant — the Foil Department Supervisor. I asked her one of my "crazy" questions: *"Would you be willing to stop the production line on each shift? So I can tell them about this new business — why we're doing it, and the profit challenge we now face? We could even serve them all five products, in advance of their release, so they can actually taste the difference we're trying to make!"*

Sometimes corporate "craziness" is contagious! ☺ She said *"Let's DO it!"* It might not seem like much. But in manufacturing, time is money. Aside from changeovers to other products, production lines are ONLY stopped for maintenance and repair. This was *neither*. But stop them, we did!

The workers were initially shocked. The line is stopping??? What's wrong??? What happened *next* shocked them even *more*. They came into their plant cafeteria to find the tables set with linen tablecloths and flowers.

The third shock was *my presence*. I was later told no one had ever come from "corporate" to talk to line workers about the business. Many of them had not completed high school. But they were *smart* . . . and *most* were also company shareholders. Why would they *not* care intensely about the company's success and their role in it?

So, there I stood . . . with my big stuffed chicken. Educating them for 20 minutes about our strategic business opportunity and the tactical difficulties hindering our success. Issuing them my Chicken Challenge: Anything they could do to maximize their production performance would drop right to the bottom line. Capping off the meeting with a gourmet feast!

Why was I not surprised when they shared notes with each other? *"My favorite is Chicken Dijon! What's yours?"* Why was I not surprised when they became our biggest ambassadors for these new products with their families and friends? And with the managers of their local grocery stores, asking them to stock their shelves?

And why was I not surprised when, through their personal engagement with these new products, they successfully dropped $200,000 to the bottom line through increased efficiencies and reduced waste?

These five products generated revenues of $15 million in their first 18 months on the market. Twenty years later, I was still finding them on grocery store shelves. I have never played baseball, but I've always wondered: Is *this* how it feels to hit a Grand Slam Home Run?

What an honor and privilege it was to work for that wonderful company! And to become a shareholder on my first day there. Decades later, I remain a shareholder . . . and a huge fan!

Yes, indeed... **Secret #2** is certainly true in Leadership. Information is POWER. Especially when it's used to release untapped potential, engage employees as *owners* with a personal stake in the outcome, and mobilize collective achievement.

But **Secret #2** is also true — sometimes, *ominously* so — in Life.

Facts Are Your Friends . . .
whether they're friendly or not.

a.k.a.: What you don't know *can* hurt you.
It might even kill you.

Fast Forward . . .

It took a total of ten days for science to confirm my suspicions. It was almost surreal to see, on live ultrasound, the mass that had been lurking inside my left breast. How appropriate that it would show up so *black*. So dark. So threatening.

The needle biopsy was scheduled two days out. My radiologist advised that my primary care physician would call me with the results three days later. We had already planned a weekend getaway with loved ones 1,000 miles away. Coincidence? You had taught me years earlier, Lord, there was *no such thing.*

March 4: *Your Sovereignty is amazing, Lord — so reassuring!*
The timing of this weekend trip is so perfect . . .
to get away for a few days while we await the news . . .
the chance to see dear friends. . . . Let the witnessing begin.

Three days after the biopsy, we were at a restaurant. We had just ordered lunch when my cell phone rang. My radiologist . . . <u>not</u> my primary care physician. He had just received my results and was so alarmed, he wanted me to know immediately. He asked for my doctor's phone number, so he could call her directly instead of just faxing her office.

He was kind and compassionate.
He was also crystal clear in his urgency.

March 7: *Yes, it's cancer. Invasive ductal carcinoma.*
It's extremely aggressive — a 9 on a scale of 1 to 9.
You need to get to a surgeon AS SOON AS POSSIBLE.

Ninety minutes later, I was talking with my doctor. She had already seen the pathology and spoken with the radiologist. The first words out of her mouth rocked me back:

"If this were my pathology, I would have a double mastectomy."

I couldn't help but think:
When you're "between a rock and a hard place," turn to The Rock.
He is THE Miracle Maker and THE Mover and Shaker.

I was 1,000 miles from home. Needing to get to a surgeon ASAP. But which surgeon? I had no idea *who*, but I knew immediately *where*.

Moffitt Cancer Center in Tampa, Florida. Nationally-renowned cancer research and treatment facility. Eighty miles from our home in Central Florida. But that isn't why I knew it was The Place for me to go. It was because of their kindness and generosity to the patients at Samaritan's Touch Care Center — the Labor of Love I had recently left behind.

Like many other health care providers, Moffitt had been captivated by Your vision there, Lord . . . and had donated *millions* of dollars in comprehensive cancer care to countless patients who were in desperate need of their life-saving help.

But as Executive Director, I rarely interacted with Moffitt's clinical staff. It had been over two years since I had spoken by phone with our liaison there. I prayed, *"Lord, what was her name?"* Immediately, her name popped into my mind as if on a billboard!

I called Moffitt's general number . . . but was told no such person worked there. Until the operator remembered one woman had married and changed her last name. Could it be . . . ?

I was transferred to her voicemail. It was her! But her message said she would be out of town until the following week. *"If you consider this an emergency, please leave a message for my assistant."* I did. Her assistant called me back within 15 minutes!

I explained my situation and told her why I was calling Moffitt. Adding that, as someone with insurance who could pay my share, I had made it my practice (whenever possible) to thank the volunteer providers at Samaritan's Touch with my health care business. She was blessed to hear this whole story, with its confirmation that she works for a great organization.

She transferred me to a scheduler in the Women's Center . . . who said there were NO appointments that week. The earliest was ten days out. She asked, *"Do you want that appointment?"*

Ten days? I had been told I needed to see a surgeon ASAP. I didn't know what to say . . . so I didn't say anything. I just held the phone in silence, while the scheduler waited patiently (also in silence). A long time passed.

Suddenly, she exclaimed: *"Wait a minute! I see we now have a cancellation for Thursday this week with Dr. Christine Laronga. She's head of the program."* I asked, *"What program?"* She answered, *"The Breast Program at Moffitt."*

A pretty good appointment to have . . . Amen, Lord? ☺

Just 3.5 hours after I had received my diagnosis?! An appointment, *in three days*, with the <u>head</u> of the Breast Program at Moffitt Cancer Center?! Just long enough for me to fly back to Florida and pick up my medical records?!

When we met Dr. Laronga on March 10, she asked how I had come to be sitting with her that day. I told her the whole story, adding:

> *"The Lord has clearly orchestrated this.*
> *He has ordained that you would be my surgeon.*
> *So I know He has placed me in very good hands."*

Her response left me almost breathless, Lord . . . *reassuring* me that You had Your hands *all over* my journey.

"You don't know the whole story. I wasn't supposed to be here today.
I was scheduled to be here tomorrow, but I'm going to be out of town.
I had already picked today as my substitute clinic day,
but had forgotten to tell the staff."

So, three days earlier, when I had been 1,000 miles away — silent on the phone, not knowing what to say to the scheduler — Dr. Laronga was at her computer in another part of Moffitt's complex. Typing her availability into the scheduling system. So her appointment would pop up at the <u>perfect</u> moment . . . *because it had my name on it!!!*

Now, sitting in that appointment, I realized why You had chosen her, Lord. Dr. Laronga's clinical skills and compassion put the "ribbon and bow" on the Gift of Peace You had already imparted to me.

We discussed all my options — which, as it turned out, were few. The tumor was too large for a lumpectomy. A mastectomy was a *certainty*. The only question was: One or two?

"If any of you lacks wisdom, you should ask God,
who gives generously to all without finding fault,
and it will be given to you."
(James 1:5)

I had been praying for <u>Your</u> wisdom, Lord, since the beginning of this journey. Since before I had any facts. Back when "only" my intuition was on high alert.

February 28: *I know You will meet me in my need, Lord.*
Give me Your wisdom and discernment.
Show me what You want of me.
Speak to me. You are my Beloved. I am Yours.
Do with me as You will.

Now I had *facts*. And, like **Secret #2** says:

Facts Are Your Friends . . .
whether they're friendly or not.

These facts were most certainly *not* friendly. The tumor wasn't just *large* . . . it was *aggressive*. But <u>without</u> these facts, how could *any* of us determine the best course of treatment to pursue?

Yet I also had *You*, Lord — The Great Physician *and* my <u>Best</u> Friend — answering my prayers for Your wisdom. Wisdom You confirmed, *within 72 hours of my diagnosis*. When You sent me <u>five</u> women — smart, wise women of faith — who (without conferring with each other) <u>all</u> urged me to consider a double mastectomy.

Leadership and Life are full of ups and downs. Not unlike a roller coaster, at times.

I used to love roller coasters. When I could choose which one to ride . . . and how much of a thrill I was "up for" that day. But what do we do when we reach a peak in Leadership or Life and realize that, just beyond the crest, we're heading for a freefall that will leave our stomach in our throat?

Is that where we can *really* learn what it means to
"Let Go and Let God"???

Secret #3

A Valley is A Terrible Thing to Waste.
So, make the most of it.

Flashback . . .

Isn't every Valley defined by the Mountains that surround it?

There have been numerous Valleys in my leadership career. Times when Mountains of various kinds towered over me. When I wondered whether I should try to go over, around, or through them . . . or retreat altogether. Both before — and since — I opened my heart to You, Lord.

Times when I overcame. Times when I failed.
Never without growing *a lot*.

Like at the Mountain of Betrayal . . .

. . . where I discovered that a colleague I thought trustworthy was smiling to my face while stabbing me in the back. Character assassination is nasty business. Lies whispered in secret. Undermining at every turn. This happened *twice*. Two different women, in two different companies. Years and miles apart.

Maybe I was naïve back then. I believed there was plenty of success around for everyone. Now, decades later, I *still* believe it . . . and I'm decidedly *not* naïve. I have seen it proven true time and time again.

These two colleagues apparently believed otherwise — that my success would somehow take a bite out of "their" piece of The Pie. They couldn't imagine that, *together*, we could make The Pie <u>bigger</u> and *all* have more than enough to "eat."

I can't lie. It hurt . . . deeply. But each time, I realized I was at a Choice Point. The first time, I chose well. The second time, I "fought fire with fire" and we both got burned.

The first time, I decided to just keep "being me." Trusting that, eventually, people would see my character didn't match her words. I also initiated a private "constructive confrontation," facilitated by our mutual boss.

It lasted all night long.

I wanted to understand her and look for ways we could build bridges. I declared my commitment: Despite her past choices, I would continue to do everything *I* could to support her success going forward. I meant it. She wanted no part of it. I did it anyway.

But something <u>did</u> change that day. She now knew that <u>I</u> knew. Her hidden agenda was out in the open. And people eventually <u>did</u> see the truth . . . about *both* of us.

She lost credibility and left the company. I was promoted.

I didn't know You then, Lord. So, I was ill-equipped to touch the soul wounds that had lured her into believing Lies. Like the Lie that "Success" was all about Win-Lose, so others — especially females? — must be enemies. Maybe someday, I will have the chance tell her about You, Lord . . . and the Hope and Healing that *only You* can bring. Maybe she already knows.

Years later, with the second colleague, I grew weary of the constant battle. The relentless opposition to every business strategy or project I put forward. Her opposition to me became *predictable.* Others saw it, too, but didn't call her on it. At least, not openly. There was a final "straw" and I was the proverbial "camel" with a backache.

I decided to recruit an ally. A new colleague who knew nothing about the history . . . until *I* told him, behind closed doors. Painting myself as a Victim. Not recognizing I had also become a Victimizer.

I'm not proud of it. He was uneasy; rightly so. He went to a trusted confidant – a corporate friend of mine. I was called out in a very visible, humiliating way. Humiliating, because I was wrong... and, deep down, I *knew* it. It wasn't who I wanted to be. And it gave me no comfort that my self-appointed nemesis was called out, too.

> *"Wounds from a friend can be trusted . . ."*
> (Proverbs 27:6)

It was the best thing that could have happened to me. It made me take a good look in the mirror. My character grew *a lot*, albeit *painfully.*

You were just starting to make Your way onto my radar screen back then, Lord. Getting my attention. You and I have come a <u>long</u> way since then. Thankfully, I never made *that* mistake again. Maybe someday, I'll even get the chance to apologize to her.

Yes, Lord. Betrayal is a knife that cuts deep . . . emotionally and professionally. It can embody a powerful combination of Crisis and Opportunity. And isn't that Opportunity magnified — even *exponentially* — whenever we accept and fully capitalize on **Secret #3**?

A Valley is A Terrible Thing to Waste.
So, make the most of it.

But what about when it is our own *body* that betrays us?

Funny how *this* betrayal is *also* a knife that cuts deep. This time, emotionally and *physically.* Bringing along its own powerful blend of Crisis and Opportunity.

Fast Forward . . .

How could I "make the most of" such a grueling Valley, Lord? The radical cutting away of parts of my body so closely aligned with my femininity? The difficult treatments sure to follow? The temporary side effects and, more importantly, the permanent consequences? After 59 years without *any* major health issues or major surgeries of *any* kind?

I can't do *anything* apart from You. (John 15:5)
But *with* You? *Nothing* can stop me! (Matthew 19:26)

Is that why You kept building up my *spirit*, Lord? So I would be able to withstand the imminent "tearing down" of my body? Like with the scheduling of my surgery . . .

. . . which was no less miraculous than the choice of my surgeon.

I had prayerfully decided not only on a double mastectomy, but also on breast reconstruction. Making this decision right up front — no pun intended! ☺ — would actually spare me one additional surgery.

Dr. Laronga wanted a certain plastic surgeon to assist her. Someone she considered "the best" for my case — Dr. Paul Smith. The wait for him could take up to six weeks. My husband was *urgently* concerned — insistent that the surgery be scheduled ASAP before this aggressive cancer could spread.

I tried to reassure him:

"Look at how the Lord <u>miraculously</u> confirmed my appointment with the
<u>head</u> of Moffitt's Breast Program just 3.5 hours after my diagnosis.
Do you think the Lord of the Universe could <u>also</u>
orchestrate my <u>surgery</u> at the time He considers <u>perfect</u>?"

I even went so far as to say:

"This is major surgery, which is always risky. I could die on the table.
I'm not saying I'm having a premonition or would <u>want</u> that,
but it's possible.

If the Lord knows He's going to take me Home during the surgery,
and He wants to schedule it in six weeks instead of four,
that just means whatever work He has left for me to do
will take six weeks instead of four.
We need to trust <u>Him</u> to work out <u>His</u> plan in <u>His</u> perfect timing."

A few days later, the surgery scheduler called.

"I'm calling you with a surgery date of April 4. [Only 2.5 weeks out!]
I must tell you . . . It's <u>very</u> <u>unusual</u> for us to schedule surgery like this
before the patient has met with the plastic surgeon.
We're obviously doing it in this case, but I'll be honest with you . . .
I have no idea why."

I said:

"I know why. I am a woman of Faith.
And I have been praying the Lord would schedule this
in <u>His</u> perfect timing."

She answered:

"Well, <u>I</u> will tell <u>you</u> that I have been here nine years, and that is
the ONLY reason this surgery has been scheduled this quickly!"
. . . adding . . . "By the way, I agree with you!" ☺

And I will never forget my encounter with a nurse practitioner just days before my "date" with the OR, as she reviewed all my test results and helped finalize my preparations.

April 2: She asked, "How are you?" I said, "Fine . . . I'm really fine."
She said, "It's the ones who tell me they're fine that scare me."
I realized she thought I must be in denial about the gravity of it all.
I said, "Oh, no . . . Let me tell you <u>why</u> I really am FINE."

I told her about <u>You</u>, Lord . . . Who You are, what You mean to me,
how I trust You, even in this wilderness . . .
how I have asked You to have Your way and "milk it"
for all it's worth to You, for Eternity's sake.

I told her my Joy and Peace are not dependent on my circumstances,
they are dependent on my relationship with You.

Then she hugged me. Not the brief "pat on the back" hug
one offers as a moment of comfort. It was a long, clinging hug . . .
the kind of hug you know is trying to embrace a Truth as its own.
She looked in my eyes and said, "You are so sweet."
I said, "No . . . HE is sweet." She hugged me again . . . long and hard.

Oh, Lord . . . You have taught me so much about Valley travel. Life is real and raw. Often, brutally so. We can't escape it, much as we might want to try. Whatever comes our way, we must *deal* with it . . . and learn to truly LIVE, no matter what.

How do we do that in a way that enables us to "make the most" of whatever Valley Reality we are in? It's crucial that we *reframe* that Reality . . . isn't it, Lord? Not *deny* it. Rather, learn to look at it *differently.*

Through Your eyes . . . and the "lens" of Your Word.

That nurse practitioner's hug told me *so much* . . . about the "bigger picture" within which my Valley trek was occurring.

April 8: It's such a picture of the world today, Lord . . .
with all the turmoil, uncertainty, anxieties and fears
that seem inevitable in a world that is "out of control" on so many levels.
People are desperate to know that You are REAL, You are ALIVE,
and You are moving with Power and Grace and Love
on behalf of those who are desperate for Your Touch . . .
which includes ALL of us, whether we know it or not.

Oh, Lord . . . Sometimes, try as we might, there seems to be no way to put a positive "spin" on what we are facing. A Valley *is* a *terrible* thing. Wouldn't we all agree? Maybe that's why **Secret #3** can seem so *impossible* on its face:

A Valley is A Terrible Thing to Waste.
So, make the most of it.

But You have a way of turning The Impossible on its head . . . don't You, Lord? Even when we don't yet have eyes to see You at work in our lives.

And so, my journey through the Valley of the Shadow began in earnest. The Valley I had not chosen. The Valley that was inevitable. The Valley I would not wish on anyone else.

The Valley I would now *never trade*, even if I could . . .
not for <u>any</u> worldly wealth.

Secret #4

Don't Just Fight Like a Girl.
Fight like God's Girl . . . on your knees.

Flashback . . .

You have used so many other Valleys, Lord, to humble me and refine me in the heat of adversity. Valleys where You grew me into more of the leader — the *person* — You have created and called me to be. Valleys where You made it abundantly clear that my strongest "fighting" position was on my knees.

Like the Valley at the Mountain of Addiction . . .

. . . where You led me to consult extensively with a company President whose suspected alcoholism was wreaking havoc on his organization. The anonymous letter sent to his boss — the CEO — was chilling in both its accusations and threats. Long, binging lunches. Loud, belligerent leadership. Lewd, belittling liaisons. Without solutions, the next letter would go to the city's major newspaper.

I had never been faced with an executive coaching challenge of this magnitude before — with such grave personal and corporate consequences. I had no idea how to "take on" this deadly addiction in the life of one who had the leverage to make so many people's lives miserable.

But You knew . . . didn't You, Lord? I wore out my knees in prayer — seeking You on behalf of this struggling President and his struggling people. Asking for Your direction and mercy . . . Your grace and power. And You led me, every step of The Way.

A funny thing happened as we traveled through this Valley together. That special, priceless thing You love to do . . . whenever You are inviting <u>me</u> into another season of *personal* (and, often, radical) Transformation. You held up a mirror to <u>me</u> . . . and I saw my <u>own</u> addiction.

Authenticity has been one of my core values for as long as I can remember. Always being willing to ask myself the same questions I am asking others to answer. Always seeking to "walk my talk." So I am not defaulting to the pale counterfeit of leadership that asserts: "Do as I say, not as I do." Not always *succeeding* at Authenticity, perhaps . . . but always *seeking* it.

The more I sought solutions for this corporate leader who had lost his way — Big Time! — the more I saw the ugliness of my *own* problem. And the more I realized I, too, was a leader of great influence who was quickly losing *her* way. You could have led me to <u>any</u> client, Lord. But You had led me to <u>this</u> client. For such a time as this. Not only to *help* . . . but to *be helped*.

It grieves me to say this President eventually balked and refused my most significant recommendation — the clinical evaluation I was convinced he needed. It didn't help that his boss turned out to be, at best, his enabler . . . and, at worst, his drinking buddy. You taught me A LOT, Lord, about how to more *successfully* confront such tough issues in the future.

But You did *so much more* for me.

In the course of that very Spirit-directed engagement,
You delivered *me* from alcoholism.
By Your Amazing Grace, I have now been
free from that bondage for *26 years!*

Decades later, the Valley at the Mountain of Persecution
was no less transformational.

Shortly before my retirement, Samaritan's Touch came under severe attack. Two attorneys opposed some of our funding. Going so far as to threaten the decision-makers with *personal* and *criminal liability* if they approved our grant. Pledging to withdraw their opposition to us "if only" we would take Jesus Christ out of our mission, logo, materials and practices.

Is that all???

You gave me the privilege, Lord — *and the courage* — to stand firm in the face of those threats. And to testify about You . . . with gentleness and respect, as Your Word says. In very public, even televised, settings.

This was a high-stakes encounter. The funding was *significant* for us. Yet I couldn't help but think there was <u>another</u> reason You had allowed these attacks, Lord. Like the conversations that were provoked (behind closed doors) among countless people of influence. Wrestling with questions like:

What is the legitimate role of Christian faith in our community?
What would *any* of us risk, if asked to *deny* You?

I have always liked the expression "Fight like a Girl." We "girls" are *strong*, after all. And determined. ☺ But **Secret #4** takes these truths to another level altogether. Because *no one* is stronger or more determined than *You*, Lord. Nor more able to win *any* battle . . . against <u>all</u> odds.

Don't Just Fight Like a Girl.
Fight like God's Girl . . . on your knees.

After months of battle, our grant was *unanimously approved!*

I retired from Samaritan's Touch just weeks later, Lord. Grateful that You had "made the most" of <u>that</u> Valley in ways far beyond what I could have ever imagined. Knowing You had used that very public crucible to strengthen Your people throughout our whole *county* . . . for the trials we would (and will) *all* face in the coming days.

"Consider it pure joy . . . whenever you face trials of many kinds,
because you know that the testing of your faith produces perseverance.
Let perseverance finish its work, so that you may be
mature and complete, not lacking anything."
(James 1:2-4)

What if I had caved, Lord? As many had *encouraged* me to do, out of their fear over the threatened loss of funds? If I had taken that "easier" route, would I have even noticed that my faith had atrophied? Instead, You *strengthened* my faith. Not just for the present battle, but for the one I had no inkling was just around the next bend . . .

. . . at the Mountain of Cancer.

Is that why it's called "the Valley of the Shadow," Lord?
Because this Mountain towers above all others?

Fast Forward . . .

Thanks to You, Lord, a dear Forever Brother — Pastor Ray! — suggested I set up a free, Caring Bridge web page (www.caringbridge.org). It would be a less taxing way to keep everyone updated on my progress. I had never *heard* of such a thing, but thought: What a great idea!

So, two days before my surgery, I created my page and briefly recounted the "saga" that had led me to that point. I had no idea at the time how this simple act would so quickly unleash a life-*sustaining* "avalanche" of prayer . . . from all around the world!

Then, just 28 days after my diagnosis, I was wheeled into the OR . . . and the only "me" I had ever known was changed forever.

In the presence of the only One who *never* changes.

April 5: *From the moment I awoke yesterday,*
I felt like I was in a cocoon . . . surrounded by Your embrace, Abba.

No fear, no anxiety . . . only assurance of
Your nearness, Your love, Your divine protection.
This was not an intellectual concept . . .
It was a physical sensation of Your Presence.
Words fail me . . .

"*Be still, and know that I am God.*"
(Psalm 46:10)

The immediate results were *so encouraging!*

First, I survived the surgery! (Most of me, at least). ☺ The tumor was large, but had not invaded the skin or the chest wall . . . so they got it all. The right breast was apparently clean. The "sentinel node" was actually four nodes clustered together. All were cancer free, so they left other lymph nodes in place. The surgical pathology report (analyzing hundreds of slices) would come the following week. But my surgeon was well-pleased, as were we.

Anesthesia, pain meds and I didn't get along, however. I finally kept some chicken broth down. I still needed even more physical nourishment to catch up with the awesome *spiritual* nourishment *You* had fed me, Lord. Through the "powerful and effective" prayers of the *hundreds* of saints you were already mobilizing on my behalf!

Some of that Nourishment, though, was much closer to home. <u>You</u> are the Bread of Life, after all . . . aren't You, Lord?

April 6: *The tech on my floor came in yesterday at 4:15 AM*
to take my vitals. We ended up having "church" for 45 minutes
— praising You, Lord, together!!!
She told me she had first come into my room at 1:00 AM.
I was sound asleep. She said she felt Peace filling the room
and thought to herself, "This patient must be a Jesus-follower."
She said she could tell from Your Presence in the room.
Goosebumps, Amen?!

My discharge from the hospital two days later — Woo Hoo! — was followed by other not-so-pleasurable discharges. (Enough said?! ☺) Especially, perhaps, those that came through the drains hanging out of my chest . . . which had to be "stripped" daily for the first two weeks.

My new full-time job was Recovery from Surgery — Step 1 of my treatment plan. Step 2 was coming, although its magnitude had not yet been determined. So, I focused on climbing out of <u>this</u> part of The Valley . . . one breath at a time.

> April 10: *I have learned several things that are worth noting:*
> *1) Pain meds (when used appropriately) are a BLESSING!*
> *2) There is a fine line between doing enough and doing too much.*
> *Don't cross that line!!! Patience is a virtue!!!*
> *3) Love is (as the song says) "a many-splendored thing."*
> *What a blessing it is to have my husband watching out for me*
> *with such loving concern and protection!*
> *4) A warm, cuddly kitty (curled up between my legs*
> *during a long sleepless night) is a special brand of medicine!*
> *5) You are The Great Physician, Lord. You still (always) make house calls.*
> *And You never take even a moment "off"!!!*
> *6) We truly CAN do ALL things through Christ who strengthens us!!!*

When we can't move much without excruciating pain, we realize how much time the mind has to work its magic . . . or mayhem. Every moment becomes a Choice Point — an opportunity to give in to the darkness or grab hold of The Light. When our thoughts become a constant internal conversation, *what* we say to ourselves becomes all the more *vital*.

Do we choose to speak Life… or death? We need to choose well.

> April 11: *Good morning, Lord! HAPPY MONDAY!!!*
> *Much of the world groans on Monday, thinking*
> *"Do I have to go (to work, school, etc. . . . .)?"*
> *You change everything, Lord!!!*
> *You're the best "multivitamin" never "invented" — Vitamin J.C.!!!*

And You have a way of turning even slang into something POWERFUL!
Like "TGIF." The world says, "Thank goodness it's Friday!"
Sadly, so many believe weekdays must be endured . . .
until the "promise" of the weekend is fulfilled (or not).
YOU, Lord, transform those four simple letters (TGIF)
into a life-transforming Rx: "Today God Is First!!!"
If only we declared that — with passion! — all seven days each week . . .
What a difference it would make in our lives!!!

Sometimes You calm the storm raging around us, Lord.
Sometimes You calm us in the middle of the storm.
Either way is a testimony to Your
Amazing Grace and Life-Altering Power!!!

The surgery was now behind me, but this Valley marathon was far from over. I had four short weeks to recover before the next stage of treatment would begin in earnest. My surgeon had mentioned the "C" word — Chemo — as highly likely, but the final determination would depend on the detailed pathology.

I kept hearing the "C" word *You* were whispering, Lord . . .

"For to me, to live is Christ and to die is gain."
(Philippians 1:21)

The four weeks passed like a blur. The drains came out. The incisions began to heal. My strength rebounded. The pain subsided . . . the *physical* pain, at least.

As an amateur photographer, one of my favorite subjects is landscapes. I am so thankful I don't have any photos of my physical "landscape" back then. There is no sugar-coating the image I saw in the mirror when I looked at my battle-scarred body. It's an image I'd just as soon forget.

Maybe that's why I kept holding so tightly to Your "C" word, Lord. It kept reminding me that all You *ever* saw was the *whole* me.

The *real* me.

"The Lord does not look at the things people look at.
People look at the outward appearance,
but the Lord looks at the heart."
(1 Samuel 16:7)

How could I know then, Lord . . .
that this Truth would become even *more dear* to me . . .

. . . or that **Secret #4** . . .

Don't Just Fight Like a Girl.
Fight like God's Girl . . . on your knees.

. . . would become even more crucial for me
in the difficult months still to come?

Secret #5

Don't Just Believe What You See.
Believe what you know . . .
and you will have eyes to see it.

Flashback . . .

Funny how Opportunity comes knocking . . . often (usually?) at the most Unexpected Times and in the most Unexpected Ways.

I had begun my career in the nonprofit sector. At one point, spending years at a Voluntary Action Center. Matching the talents of thousands of volunteers with the unmet needs of thousands in our community.

I loved my job, the people I worked with, and the people I served.
I guess it showed.

I had just finished a presentation at a communitywide meeting when a corporate recruiter approached me. *"There's an opening at _____. You really should apply."* I was flattered. I thanked him, but told him the truth: *"I love my job . . . and I'm not looking to make a change."*

Just weeks later, after a *different* presentation in the community, a *different* corporate recruiter approached me about the same position.

"There's an opening at _____. You really should apply." Opportunity knocking twice? Maybe I should at least check it out . . .

My career in Corporate America was launched. The Human Resources function at Blue Cross & Blue Shield of Florida, a 3,100-employee company. Starting at the bottom, eager to live out what I believed (what, sadly, is only a cliché to many):

People really *are* the most important asset in *any* company.

By then, I was a devotee of the Human Potential Movement. I believed people could BE and DO anything they *wanted* to BE and DO. What untapped potential was waiting to be unleashed in this large company?! I jumped into every new challenge with both feet — growing in experience, confidence, wisdom . . . and the trust of my internal clients.

Training and Development. Designing and delivering the company's first comprehensive Management and Supervisory Training Program. Workshops in every aspect of how to get the best possible results working *with* and *through* the people producing those results.

Organization Development. Mobilizing Two-way Communication between management and employees. Facilitating interdepartmental team building and problem-solving. Coaching executives in how to develop a more people-empowering culture.

I loved my job, the people I worked with, and the people I served.
I guess it showed.

The President of the company called me into his office one day. He wanted to make me Director of Personnel. (I would become only the fourth female to date at the Director level). I remarked, *"There is someone already sitting in that chair."* He said, *"I want to put you there."*

The President was fed up. The function had lost its internal credibility. So, line executives were going *around* it — doing their own hiring. Spending "mega-dollars" that were unbudgeted. Making poor hiring decisions. Putting the company at risk.

He wanted to fire everyone and start from scratch. A chance to choose and build my *own* team from the ground up? Tempting . . . but I said "No." I wanted to see what the *current* team was "made of." I couldn't help but believe there was hidden potential just waiting — *longing* — to be found and released.

And I wanted the chance to prove it.

I agreed to accept the opportunity IF — and *only* if — the President would agree to give me the time I wanted for my "experiment." One year. He said, *"Go for it . . . and keep me informed."*

That's when I first became enamored with "The Butterfly Effect." How a butterfly can transform itself — and the world — so dramatically. A nondescript earthbound caterpillar becomes a strikingly-beautiful winged creature much stronger than it looks. One flap of its wings sets in motion a distant hurricane.

I told my new team the truth. If it were up to the President, they would all be history. But I had cut a deal. We *all* had one year to prove him wrong.

You had been so generous to me, Lord. (Me, who was still so *totally* clueless about You). My credibility throughout the company was wide and deep. Now, I would do everything in *my* power to give my teammates every opportunity to succeed. But it was up to *them* to step into — and *up* to — those opportunities.

Changing behavior is not an overnight proposition. It takes determination and a lot of hard work. Mostly, of course, it takes *You*, Lord . . . especially for deep, lasting change. My ignorance about You back then was exceeded only by my lack of interest in seeking You.

But that's another story . . .

I and my team were determined. We *all* worked *really hard*. I told them I would believe in them… until *they* proved me wrong.

I sought candid feedback about each of my team members from executives and managers throughout the company. I shared that feedback one-to-one . . . even as I asked my team to share with me *their* frustrations and hopes for the future.

Together, we established individual development plans, plus strategic and tactical plans to help transform the function — and my team — from liabilities into assets. And *together*, we worked those plans.

Success *abounded* — for Personnel <u>and</u> for my team. I was privileged to be their coach, but they earned those "wins." Almost *all* of them blossomed into high potential, results-producers. One eventually became a corporate VP.

<u>Secret #5</u> had proven, once again, to be true:

Don't Just Believe What You See.
Believe what you know . . . and you will have eyes to see it.

But is this an even harder "sell" in the Valley of the Shadow?

Fast Forward . . .

April 19: *Passover officially began.*
I am mindful of (and grateful for) the Lamb of God
and Your grace in "passing over" all
that would keep me separated from You.
So now, I am waiting in the stillness . . .
for healing, strength, nourishment . . .
for Hope to reign . . .
You are in the action, Lord . . . and the stillness . . .
in the fire . . . and the ashes . . .
in the pain . . . and the relief . . .
in the morning fog . . . and the sparkling sunshine . . .
in the cocoon . . . and the butterfly . . .
YOU ARE . . . and that is more than enough.

About two weeks after my surgery, the other "shoe" dropped. I met my oncologist, Dr. Susan Minton. I liked her a lot — thorough, very forthcoming with information and risk factors. The "Good, Bad and Ugly" of my clinical picture. Discussed with great sensitivity.

The bottom line? Because of the size of the tumor and its aggressiveness, the entire Tumor Board at Moffitt — comprised of some fifty cancer specialists (surgeons, oncologists, radiologists, etc.) — *unanimously* recommended aggressive chemotherapy. The "Big Guns" (as I later came to call them).

Why? The Aggression Factor. This particular cancer's apparent "mission" — I learned early on *not* to call it *"my"* cancer, as if I was claiming ownership of it — was to leave its place of origin and search for another "home" in my body. Although the lymph nodes were clear, the likelihood that rogue cells had broken off and were circulating around was high.

> Fighting *probabilities* . . . not *certainties*.
> Maybe one day we'll know for sure.
> And not have to just bet the odds.

The plan? Hit those phantom cells *fast* and *hard*. Condensing a six-month regimen of powerful chemo "cocktails" into just over three months. Beginning May 5 — just four weeks after surgery, allowing my body to regain strength. After all, except for this cancer "blip," I was very healthy . . . so they thought I could tolerate it.

> That old joke came to mind:
> *"Aside from that, Mrs. Lincoln, how did you enjoy the play?"* ☺

In addition, I would be given Neulasta shots for the first half of the treatment cycle. To rebuild my white blood cells. Boost my immune system. Reduce the chance of infection. Longer term, the oral chemo medications many women take would not be an option for me. Since the cancer was "triple negative" — only 15-20% are — no such meds were yet available.

> Hence, the treatment plan — hit *fast* and *hard*.

April 21: Lord, I (and many others) have asked that
You give these doctors Your supernatural wisdom and discernment
leading to today's recommendations. I believe You have done just that.
Their conclusions were <u>strong</u>. No "waffling."

Help me prepare — body, mind, emotions and spirit —
for all <u>You</u> see ahead that is still invisible to me.
I cannot do this, Lord. Only You can.
So I will claim Your Word as true . . . knowing You <u>are</u> Truth!
You are my dear Abba, and I rest in Your loving care.

Once again, Opportunity came knocking . . . at the most Unexpected Time, in the most Unexpected Way.

On April 29, a week before chemo was to begin, a Forever Sister (Nancy) called me from another state. One of the many "stretcher bearers" You had mobilized, Lord, to carry me into Your Presence (like the paralytic in Luke 5:18-20). For healing only You could provide. You had led her to a certain passage that day and . . . she sensed it was a Word for *me*.

"I am convinced, being fully persuaded in the Lord Jesus,
that nothing is unclean in itself.
But if anyone regards something as unclean,
then for that person it is unclean . . .
Therefore do not let what you know as good be spoken of as evil . . .
May the God of Hope fill you with all joy and peace as you trust in Him,
so that you may overflow with Hope by the power of the Holy Spirit."
(Romans 14:14,16; 15:13)

The world sees chemo as Poison. It is certainly grueling . . . not for the faint-of-heart. But in light of those Scriptures, Lord, we began to look at chemo *differently*. *You* had led me to that course of treatment. *You* had also declared that Your plans were to prosper me and not harm me (Jeremiah 29:11). So, we began to believe that, by Your Divine Sovereignty, *You* would *sanctify* those chemicals — set them aside for a *sacred* purpose.

Killing whatever renegade cancer cells might exist . . .
without harming me in any way.

As I soaked in Your Word, a vision began to form in my spirit. I began to see my chemo infusions as *worship* sessions. So, that is how I prepared my heart. Praying Your Word right back to You. Voicing my faith and trust in You and *what You were about to do.*

Day 1 was the longest. I arrived early for the surgical insertion of a port in my upper chest, close to my heart. Neither my veins nor my arteries could withstand the frequency and "burn" of the chemicals to be infused in the months ahead. Following that surgery, and subsequent labs, I was cleared for the first chemo treatment.

I had arrived with my <u>own</u> "port" — my Sony Walkman and head-phones — through which I would "infuse" my *spirit* with the worship music You had helped me select.

I was ushered into a private room . . . *instead* of what I had been told to expect (a reclining chair in the open area, next to all other infusion pa-tients). The nurse was surprised: *"Just so you know, you won't be in a private room like this <u>every</u> time . . . This is <u>very</u> unusual."* [In other words, don't get used to it! ☺]. I replied,

"This is just the Lord's grace. He's being so kind to me."

The room had a comfortable recliner for my husband, and a *very* comfortable adjustable bed for me. The room was darkened, the lighting dim . . . which made it peaceful and restful. *Perfect* for the private encounter I anticipated with You, Lord.

As I began to worship, I prayed out loud (softly). Placing myself in Your hands. Trusting Your protection. Speaking Your promises. Affirming my faith that You were sanctifying those chemicals. Using them for my good. (My complete prayer is in the Appendix).

I closed my eyes and sang my heart out to You. Lifting my hands off the bed. Lost in Your Presence. Every few minutes for the next three hours, the nurse came to check on me. Gently touching my arm, saying: *"I'm so sorry to disturb you."* I replied, *"No, not at all. You do whatever you need to do. I'm just worshipping the Lord and resting in His care."*

Throughout the entire infusion, I kept repeating to her: *"I'm fine . . . I am in His care . . . in His care . . . in His care."*

I was blessed to overflowing by the beauty of my time with You, Lord. But You wanted to bless me *even more.*

Three days later, I saw a woman who had been praying for me. I hadn't told her any details. What *she* told *me* left me speechless! You gave her a vision *during the infusion . . .*

She saw me in a *private room.* In a *comfortable bed.* The room was *darkened . . .* yet, at the same time, *full of light.* Because You let her see the *angels* You had stationed around me. Then You spoke to her heart:

"Don't worry. Diana is <u>fine</u>. She is <u>in</u> <u>My</u> <u>care</u>."

Fine?! In Your care?! The *same words* of reassurance You had <u>me</u> speak during the whole infusion?! Giving meaning to **Secret #5** far beyond *anything* I could have ever imagined?!

Don't Just Believe What You See.
Believe what you know . . . and you will have eyes to see it.

"Fine" turned out to be a relative term. But Your Presence is never just "relative" . . . is it, Lord? You have <u>promised</u> to *always* be with us, to *never* forsake us. Even as You have promised we will have Trouble in Life.

Trouble, with a capital T.
(John 16:33)

There was much Trouble still ahead. The Big Guns chemo — and the reconstruction process that accompanied it — had only just begun.

Is that why **Secret #6** became such a Lifeline, Lord?

Secret #6

Laugh when you can.
Cry when you must.

Flashback . . .

What was I doing in Venezuela??? Facilitating a week-long Strategic Planning and Team Building session for the in-country leadership team of a multinational corporation???

Completely in Spanish???

It wouldn't have happened if I hadn't been *fluent* in Spanish. Or if, twenty years *earlier*, I hadn't picked Spanish as my college major and spent my junior year at the University of Madrid in Spain. Or if, for twelve years before *that*, I hadn't worked my . . . fingers?! ☺ . . . off at multiple jobs, to fulfill my childhood Dream of *going* to college.

An Unlikely Dream.

My dad left school in the eighth grade to help take care of his family. My mom graduated from high school, entering the honorable (but notoriously low-paying) career of secretary.

No one else had this Dream for me. But in the seventh grade, it burst into life *within* me. No one had the money to <u>fund</u> my Dream. But my resolve to *pursue* it became *insatiable*. I worked <u>hard</u> for — and *saved* — every penny I could get my hands on.

It was all from You, Lord . . . wasn't it?
The Dream . . . The Resolve . . . The Result.
Even though I had no clue back then that You even existed.

Bottom line?
I made it to college! And my year in Spain was *awesome!*
But it didn't start out that way.

My Dream met My Reality . . . and became My Nightmare.

I had a "Gift" for Spanish. I could mimic — easily, it seemed to me — whatever sounds I heard. It wasn't until much later that I realized the Source of that Gift was *You*, Lord. But I recognized the Gift, nonetheless . . . and joyfully *embraced* it.

After eight years of study, before ever leaving this country, I had come to believe I was fluent. *I was wrong.* Now that I was in Spain, all I heard was *noise*. And I was over 6,000 miles away from family. With no extra money to call home. I didn't know a soul. I felt *totally isolated*.

So, I chose a lifestyle that matched my feelings.

I hid in my dorm room. I cried. I beat myself up: What was I thinking??? I slept for hours at a time — in the middle of the day — hoping My Reality would somehow magically disappear. Even though I didn't believe in magic.

Until the day of my Wake-Up Call.

Actually, it was more of a Realization. I had spent the last eight years preparing for this Dream of My Lifetime. I could now *waste* this priceless opportunity . . . or *embrace* it, even as I had embraced the Gift of language that sent me there. All I had to do was *let go* of my Fear.

Fear of Making Mistakes. Fear of Appearing Foolish.

So, I <u>did</u> let go . . .
. . . and my tears turned into *Undeniable* JOY!

Many months later, I came home.
Undeniably FLUENT . . . and
Undeniably GROWN UP.

Fear is a terrible prison.
Freedom from Fear is The Key to *so many* prison doors.

So, there I was, decades later . . . poised to help this Latin American leadership team at Tupperware International break through to a new level of effectiveness.

I had done this countless times, with senior leadership teams around <u>our</u> country. As a senior partner at Maxcomm Associates — a consulting firm started by my friend and former teammate, Bill Adams. Later, as Founder and CEO of other consulting firms.

But in Spanish??? NEVER!!!

So, I will <u>never</u> forget the laughter we shared, as this team bonded more deeply and envisioned more clearly the future they were committed to creating together. I will <u>never</u> forget the tears we shared, as this team honored their leader at the close of our session with heartfelt expressions of love and respect for him. (Yes . . . he cried, too.)

And I will <u>never</u> forget the combination of adrenaline and Your Holy Spirit's presence, Lord, that made it all possible!

Maybe that's what makes **Secret #6** so fascinating.

Laugh when you can.
Cry when you must.

The Dream filled me with Joy when it was first conceived. *Achieving* The Dream required all the "blood, sweat, and tears" I could muster. For the Joy set before me, I persevered. Reality struck The Dream, threatening to kill it on the spot. But Hope had its way . . . and sent Fear packing. The Dream revived . . . *blossoming* and bearing *unexpected fruit*, even <u>decades</u> later.

Even <u>today</u>!

So, I can't help but wonder, dear Reader . . .
Is there a Dream waiting to be born (or resurrected) in *your* life?

Maybe it isn't "too late" after all . . .

Fast Forward . . .

It was the morning after my surgery. I was still a little groggy when my doctors came in for their first post-surgery briefing on my current condition and continuing prognosis.

The tumor was gone! ☺ (Along with my breasts, of course). ☹ Our plan for reconstruction was dependent on *where* they found cancer. If it had penetrated my chest wall, radiation would have been necessary before even *beginning* The Rebuilding. Adding at least one more surgery to my path back to wellness . . . if not, wholeness.

Dr. Laronga was upbeat. No cancer in the chest wall! No radiation required! So, Dr. Smith had inserted temporary "tissue extenders" under my chest muscles. Over the next few months, these would be inflated until I reached my "desired" breast size. Once there, the extenders would be replaced with permanent implants.

Sounded simple enough. But this process involved stretching muscles that had never been stretched before. I had no idea at the time how painful this reconstruction would be. Sometimes Ignorance IS Bliss . . . *thankfully*.

Dr. Smith had already inflated the extenders by the same amount as the breast tissue they had removed. Dr. Laronga lifted my hospital gown to check the incisions. What she said next put me in stitches! ☺

No, wait a minute... she had already done that! ☺
And I could honestly say it didn't *only* hurt when I laughed.
But laughter is such Good Medicine . . . isn't it, Lord?

"A happy heart makes the face cheerful,
but heartache crushes the spirit."
(Proverbs 15:13)

Dr. Laronga took one look at my re-inflated chest and said:

"I think you're going to want more."

I laughed . . . until I winced. Ouch!
And I had to admit: She was right! ☺

Why reconstruction? Maybe, in part, for my own self-image. Maybe, in part, for my husband's sake. For all those times when having a feminine profile would help take away some of the "sting" of this whole journey. Or so I hoped. It didn't turn out quite like I had imagined.

I'm happy with the *profile* part . . . at least with my clothes on. It is therapeutic, somehow, having a bit more shape to me in the aftermath of what cancer took away. Personally, I would not have initiated this route just for looks. But since I was on this "Taken-Not-Chosen" Road, I might as well grab for the gusto . . . right? ☺

It is certainly not *natural*, however. I had been warned I would have no feeling in most of my chest area. Too many nerves had to be severed in the process of removing so much tissue. I just didn't know what that numbness would *be* like . . . especially in times of intimacy. For me *or* my husband. And I had no idea these implants would feel much harder than real flesh.

"Mind Over Matter" doesn't always change the matter.
But it can *always* reframe it.
And sometimes, *that's* what matters *most*.

I'm not exactly a Bionic Woman, but I still laugh sometimes when I realize I am now a combination of Original Issue and Parts Subject to Factory Recall.

Sometimes, I still cry.

By Your Grace, Lord,
You have given me eyes to see a silver lining in every cloud.
So, I *gratefully* keep *moving forward.*

May 25: *"I have loved you with an Everlasting Love;*
I have drawn you with Unfailing Kindness. I will build you up again . . .
you will . . . go out to dance with the joyful."
(Jeremiah 31:3-4)

"[Diana] will be like a well-watered garden
and [she] will sorrow no more.
[Diana] will dance and be glad.
I will turn [her] mourning into gladness;
I will give [her] comfort and joy instead of sorrow.
I will satisfy [her] with abundance,
and [she] will be filled with My bounty."
(Jeremiah 31:12-14)

Fill my cup, Lord . . . I lift it up, Lord . . .

Admittedly, some challenges were mundane at the time . . . though significant in the end. (Pun intended!) ☺

April 9: *Today is a new day, Lord,*
to celebrate Your mercies, large and small!
Thank You for the Gift of Life You have given each of us today! You are
not only The Great Physician . . . You are also The Great Plumber!!!
No disrespect intended, Abba . . . I am just SO GRATEFUL that
my post-surgery "plumbing" is finally "on the mend" . . . Enough said!!! ☺

Other challenges were "Rites of Passage" inherent in the landscape through which I was traveling . . .

April 10: *Life, for all of us, is a marathon of sorts.*
Yesterday, I hit what my running pals have called "The Wall" . . .
that level of pain I couldn't quite get past.
It started at 2:00 PM and continued
through the night without much sleep.
Thank You, Lord, for pain meds . . .
which took enough of the "edge" off to give me some relief.
By Your grace, the "glass" is ALWAYS <u>at</u> <u>least</u> half full.

April 16: *How could such simple movements*
I used to do without thinking
seem like such giant challenges in so short a time???
Lord, thank You for Your healing touch!
Thank You for how my traumatized muscles are
responding to Your loving workouts as,
not only my Great Physician, but my Great Personal Trainer!!!
The journey of a thousand pull ups begins with a single "ouch" . . .
. . . or something like that . . . Amen? ☺

Then, there was the Chemo.

April 14: *Someone just said to me:*
"I know you're afraid."
It's so hard for people to grasp, Lord,
that You offer us a Peace that is truly not "of this world."
By Your grace, I am NOT afraid.
You have given me the <u>certainty</u> of Eternal Life with You.
I am not afraid to die, Lord.
So how could I possibly be afraid to LIVE . . .
. . . come what may?
It would be "natural" to feel fear in these circumstances.
But You are SUPERNATURAL.
"Common sense" would suggest anxiety would be a "given."
But You are UNCOMMON.

Sometimes our Valleys are such that crying is not just inevitable, it is altogether fitting and appropriate. To deny our Grief Tears and Anger Tears is to deny part of the very Reality we must face and embrace. Such tears can fill our "tub" to overflowing . . . inviting us to sink down into them, almost to the point of drowning. Making it seem like we will never laugh again.

Yet, remarkably — impossibly, it seems — Laughter can also come. Uninvited, perhaps . . . but oh-so-welcome. More often, though, I believe we must *look* for Laughter. And give ourselves permission to *experience* it . . . even in the darkest of days. Gut-wrenching, fact-defying Laughter that also takes us to the point of tears. Joy Tears that "bathe" us in a different way altogether.

Encouraging and empowering us to take
The Next Step . . . even The Next Breath.

Maybe that's part of the wonder — even the *miracle* — of **Secret #6**:

Laugh when you can.
Cry when you must.

My prayers as I entered Chemo were just like my prayers as I first entered this Valley. I asked You to have *Your* way, Lord, with even the side effects I would experience.

Knowing the months would *drag on* or *fly by* . . .
. . . depending on **Secret #6**, and the Laughter or Tears of the moment.

Trusting You had Purpose beyond my immediate understanding.

For the side effects from which You would spare me . . .
. . . and those You would not.

Secret #7

Let God Turn Your Mess into His Message.
Then become His Megaphone.

Flashback . . .

It is *exhilarating* at the top, Lord!
And sometimes, very *lonely*.

Especially for women? In that "rarified" leadership "air" occupied mostly by men? Where our "trailblazing" has taught us to work harder than most and hold our "cards" very close to the chest? Hoping to keep others from exploiting our weaknesses or taking unfair advantage?

Even more so, perhaps, for *Christian* women who lead today? Who are increasingly called to navigate "Grace-FULL-y" through stormy seas of changing cultural values? Where waves of faith-based suspicions or outright hostilities threaten (at times) to swamp us?

There is so much JOY in working hard and accomplishing Success! In *whatever* our field of endeavor may be. As leaders, we take on mantles of responsibility and influence that are as challenging as they are consequential. Making a positive difference in the lives of others while accomplishing significant results in business or ministry is an unparalleled "high."

Besides, *driving* and *striving* are highly <u>rewarded</u> in our culture
. . . both tangibly and intangibly.

Even so, sometimes all that driving and striving leaves us tired. Depleted of energy and passion. And achievement can become *over*-achievement. As if no matter how many "wins" we stack up, and no matter how *big* those wins are, they are never quite *enough*. Why is that, Lord?

Could it be that, deep down, we "know"
— i.e., *believe* in our heart-of-hearts —
that <u>we</u> are never quite *enough*?

Maybe I'm the only one. Or maybe . . . not.
Not by long shot.

I began driving and striving as a child. A child who became a statistic. Maybe before they even started keeping those statistics. Regrettably, some studies today put the number of sexually-abused girls at one in *three*. Abused, most often, by one they should be able to trust.

The Valley of All Valleys . . . for me, at least.
A few years in the making. A lifetime of overcoming.

Yes, that is another Story altogether . . .

. . . and someday, I will tell it. Although I am still traveling The Road to Healing and Wholeness, I have come *a long way*. Thanks to You, Lord. And another of Your priceless invitations: *"Come, follow Me . . . and I will take you where it is <u>impossible</u> to go on your own."*

Even to the place where The Unforgivable can be *forgiven*.
Where an Enemy can be *loved* into Your Forever Family.
And where Life can become *immeasurably more* than *extraordinary!*

You have used <u>that</u> Valley, Lord — and its decades-long aftermath — to teach me *so much* about Life *and* Leadership. Like how we can lead quite successfully *despite* the wounds we hide. Successfully . . . up to a point, at least. But not without consequences.

How much of our potential is hindered by what we hide . . .
. . . even from ourselves?

You have taught me *so much*, Lord, about how what we hide can fester and come out in ways that hurt not just *us*, but *others*. How the masks we wear can leave us feeling like impostors in our own skin. How our ways of "killing" pain may be socially acceptable, but personally (and professionally and relationally) unprofitable.

No wonder it's so lonely at the top sometimes!

And You have taught me *so much*, Lord, about HOPE! What a *treasure* it is! How it *can* be found . . . even in the most *hopeless* places. How "terminal" wounds — even those of the Heart — *can* be "impossibly" *healed*. How Purpose is present even in our pain.

How Truth can *set us free* from the prison of our lies.
When *You* come, Lord . . . as The Key of all keys.

"What He opens no one can shut,
and what He shuts no one can open."
(Isaiah 22:22)

Although I have been considered a leader since I was in my teens, I'm one of those "late bloomers" spiritually. I didn't open my heart to You, Lord, until I was almost 36 years old. When, thankfully, *You came after me*. In *very personal* ways. "Goosebump" kinds of ways that made this radical feminist and hardened agnostic take notice.

Ways that became *unmistakable* and *irresistible*.
Oh, Lord, how I love sharing those stories!
Whenever You open *those* doors . . . ☺

I have been on The Adventure of My Lifetime ever since You first walked through the door of *my* heart, Lord. I'm much older now . . . and a whole lot wiser, thanks to You.

Maybe that's why You are giving me the privilege of coaching Christian Women of Influence. Mostly business owners, executives and community leaders. Leaders who, like me, want to increase our impact for You in the world . . . even as You increase the quality of our lives.

Maybe that's why You are orchestrating so many opportunities for me to speak. To share messages of Hope and Courage. In a world where Hope is increasingly hard to find . . . and where Courage is increasingly necessary to *thrive*.

Maybe that's why You are helping me finally publish this book. Because there is Victory to be found in *every* Valley. If we know where to look . . . and the One who can help us *see*. And if *we* have found The Way *through*, maybe we can help *others* find it, too.

Isn't that the very "heart" of <u>Secret #7</u>?

Let God Turn Your Mess into His Message.
Then become His Megaphone.

Someone "out there" has Messes not unlike my own . . . and needs to hear the Messages *You* have entrusted to *me*. I am only *one* of Your Megaphones, Lord . . . but I am *one*.

Which begs The Question:

What Messages have been entrusted to *you*, dear Reader . . .
. . . to be shared with those *you* have been called to influence?
And inspire?

Fast Forward . . .

Who coined the phrase "Side Effects," Lord? As if whatever happens is of a peripheral nature. Off to the side . . . not The Main Deal. When, in fact, these effects are not peripheral at all. Because when they come, they affect our whole body, mind, emotions and spirit.

Sometimes for The Good. ☺ Most times . . . not so much.

Like NAUSEA.

The doctors expected I would have it "Big Time." A predictable effect of Big Guns Chemo. They wanted to prevent it. I was slender to begin with, and they didn't want me losing any weight. Besides . . . my blood counts needed to be *boosted*, not depleted.

The doctors prescribed three powerful anti-nausea medications I was to take every day. To help me weather the storm.

I never took a single pill!

Granted, I wasn't *hungry* for months. But my taste buds, though muted, were still mostly intact. And without *any* sensation of nausea *at all*, I was willing and able to eat *every day*.

The doctors were shocked. They couldn't understand it, much less explain it. How I enjoyed every opportunity You gave me, Lord, to *help* them understand . . . it was because of You!

Then HAIR LOSS.

My doctors were right about that one.
Within two weeks, it was all gone.

May 21: *I have to admit, Lord . . .*
If I had to choose between one of two side effects,
I MUCH prefer losing my hair to having nausea!!!
The hair thing has already been a source of great laughter
(the "Wig Party" with my Sistas Elle, Moddie and Debbie!).
It's hard to imagine having a "Nausea Party" with the same feel to it . . . ☺

It wasn't all Fun and Games, of course.

Hair (for women *and* men) is an important part of our "image" to the world. An expression of our uniqueness, our personality. We express ourselves through the hairstyles we choose. Even the colors . . . although I have never colored my hair. I have quipped — with meaning far beyond these words — that I "earned" every one of my gray hairs and I'm not willing to cover them up.

They're part of My Story.

I wasn't surprised when I lost my hair. You had given me a dream weeks earlier, Lord. Two startlingly-different images. Prisoners in a concentration camp. A newborn baby.

I reflected on the first image cautiously, with great reverence. I cannot fathom the enormity of the suffering there. The conditions more horrific than any I have ever known. But I *have* been in a "prison" of a different kind. Devoid of <u>all</u> hope. It, too, was an *agonizing* place to live . . . and almost die. I, too — in my own unique way — had a very real experience of Hell.

But that's another story . . .

I <u>loved</u> the image of the newborn baby, Lord! And understood right away its Truth. First and foremost, I am *Your child*. <u>Totally</u> dependent on You. For every breath and every need. My Forever Father — my *Daddy* — who *loves* me and *will* take care of me. Regrettably, I did not have that relationship with my earthly father. After *many* years of healing, I now have it with *You*.

And I am forever grateful to finally be a "Daddy's girl"
. . . *Abba's Girl.*

"God sent the Spirit of His Son into our hearts,
the Spirit who calls out, 'Abba, Father.'
So you are no longer a slave, but God's child . . . "
(Galatians 4:6-7)

One of my favorite treasures from this season, Lord, is a photo. A portrait of two precious Forever Brothers — Paul and Richard — on either side of me. Three Christian "cue balls." (☺) In truth, three *bald eagles* — who helped bring one of my favorite Scriptures to life:

"Those who hope in the Lord will renew their strength.
They will soar on wings like eagles;
they will run and not grow weary, they will walk and not be faint."
(Isaiah 40:31)

Then came PAIN . . .
a live-in companion that overstayed its welcome.

Surgical Pain came and went, as if on a timeshare "vacation." Three times, with each of my three surgeries. The Muscle Pain of breast inflation, like an intermittent "rental." Coming every two weeks, like clockwork. Staying for several days. Over several months. No biggie, though. It only hurt when I breathed. ☺ Bone Pain "squatting" for months . . . defying eviction.

Historically, I rarely had headaches . . . and even *more* rarely, took aspirin. I learned very quickly to heed the doctors' advice. Big Guns Surgery, followed so quickly by Big Guns Chemo <u>and</u> Big Guns Reconstruction, taxes the body *Big Time.* So, *take* the Big Guns Pain Meds when needed. To break the grip of constant tension. So the body can *rest* and *sleep* . . . and *heal.*

ISOLATION was, perhaps, the worst side effect.
Or maybe, *the BEST???*

Once Chemo began, it hammered my immune system. The docs gave me strict orders: Stay at home! No visitors! To avoid infection and not slow down my treatment <u>or</u> recovery. Between Chemo and the first two of three surgeries, this relative isolation lasted *seven months.*

Tough to the max . . .
for a touchy-feely, "people person" like me. ☺

My only "Get Out of Jail" card gave me permission to go to church *one hour* every Sunday. But . . . Stay away from people! No hugging! No kissing! I grabbed the offer like a lifeline.

By Your Amazing Grace, Lord, *I only missed one Sunday!*
Yet who was encouraged <u>more</u> . . . me or the congregation? ☺

But the *real* Lifeline came during the *other* 167 hours each week. The *many* hours I spent with *You*, Lord . . . when You were the only One in the room with me. During those many hours, I grabbed hold of You like I never had before.

The *fruitfulness* of that time with You
was made evident by *The Avocado Miracle.*

We have an avocado tree right next to our home of 16 years. The tree has seen better days. It still bears the scars of past hurricanes and lightning strikes. But *that* year, our tree produced a harvest *far greater* than *any* we had ever seen. I gave up counting after 200!

We did not fertilize that tree with *anything* . . . much less, "Miracle Gro." But *You*, Lord — the One who *made* that tree — made it *miraculously* grow. *That year.* Not the year before or any year earlier. Not *since.* Just *that* year — the year I traveled through the Valley of the Shadow.

Why did You do it, Lord? I didn't *ask* You for it. You just *did it* . . . because You *can.* Then You gave me *eyes to see* what You had done. So, I would be *encouraged* to the point of AWE. And I would *thank You* and *praise You* even more!

There I was . . . ready to go to Alaska. You not only took me into a *different* "wilderness," You made me *homebound* for seven months. Where I could soak in Your Word, Your Presence, Your Living Water. Where You could fill my cup to *overflowing* . . . day after day after day.

And there was this scrawny, unfertilized avocado tree. Planted right next to our home… and all that Living Water You were pouring out. Producing a *supernaturally abundant harvest.* As if You were saying to *me*, in a very tangible and personal way:

"Press on, Daughter! There is MUCH LIFE ahead!
By My Grace, I will make you fruitful

FAR beyond your expectations and abilities...
All for My Glory!"

Isn't that a word for all of us, Lord?
And isn't that the *real* message behind **Secret #7**?

Let God Turn Your Mess into His Message.
Then become His Megaphone.

The chemo ran its course. Other side effects came and went. My chest was finally fully-inflated. (Thank you, I think?!) ☺ Subsequent surgeries completed the "permanence" and "look" of my new breasts.

I could see Light at the end of this long tunnel. It became clear that You weren't taking me Home, Lord . . . at least, not yet. Which begged another Question.

The Inevitable Question we *all* must ask.
At major points of transition in Leadership *and* Life.

The Question that, up until that moment,
I hadn't permitted myself to even *think* about . . .
much less *dream* about.

WHAT'S NEXT?

What's Next?

There's <u>always</u> something . . .
. . . somewhere.

Flashback...

Some people have the privilege of staying in one company their whole careers. Forging results and relationships that last a lifetime. I, like many others, took a different path.

First, I chased Opportunity. Later, Love chased *me*.

I will never forget the words of two of my trusted mentors. One was our company's President. The other, a former CEO of Fairchild Industries, soon to become my professor at the MBA Program at Georgetown University.

MBA??? Where did *that* notion come from?

I was not the typical MBA student. I had been climbing career ladders for eleven years since graduating from college, and was nearing a top "rung" in my present company. But I decided it was time to go to graduate school.

In my long-term career Vision, I would one day be advising *many* business owners and CEOs. I had been on the *people* side of the business (Human Resources). I also needed to be on the *profit* side of the business. With P&L responsibility. So future clients would know whatever wisdom I brought to the table came out of my *experience*, not just a book I had read.

In the 1980s, the MBA was the "must have" ticket
for the train I wanted to board.

I told my mentor, the President, what I was thinking. He said I could stay where I was. He would send me to an Executive MBA program and give me the line management positions I would need to make my way to The Top of *that* company. But if I wanted to open my opportunities *beyond* that one company, he agreed: The MBA was the way to go.

I did. So, I went . . . with his blessing.

But an MBA??? A highly quantitative degree at a major university? For someone like me, who had suffered from "Numbers-phobia" since high school? Or, at least, since I had been mercilessly ridiculed by my high school Algebra teacher? [Yes, Teachers of the World — you *do* make a difference! For better or worse . . .]

But I had been an Overcomer my whole life. Wasn't The Key to Success 10% inspiration and 90% *perspiration*? At least, that's what I told the Admissions people at Georgetown as I tried talking my way into graduate school. As I *succeeded* in talking my way into graduate school . . .

. . . where later, I graduated Number 2 in my class!
Number 2 by just *three 100ths of a point.*

But who's counting? ☺

Nearing graduation, I had already been offered a *great* position at General Foods Corporation — #39 of the Fortune 500 companies. Another one of those "Opportunities of A Lifetime." Heady stuff for a "bootstrap" gal like me, whose career had already surpassed my parents' highest and wildest expectations.

Or what they *would* have been, if they had still been alive.
Another story, indeed . . .

But this Opportunity wasn't a "no brainer." Because I was *in Love*. And this Love, who had his own highly successful career, wasn't willing to follow me to New York.

Go figure! ☺

Enter, my Mentor/Professor. He was a bottom-line kind of guy. A vital competency for an aviation executive. Maybe that's why his advice surprised me.

He said, for *all* of us, the Great Opportunities afforded by many jobs — even multiple *careers* — will come and go. But finding the person we want to spent the rest of our *life* with? That doesn't happen every day.

He had been "bitten" by the Love Bug, too.
Decades earlier.

I said "no" to General Foods and "yes" to McCormick.

Funny how things work out. Years earlier, as I had envisioned future career options, I had asked myself: *"Is there any company I would never want to work for?"* For me, the answer was simple: A tobacco company.

My dad had smoked three packs of cigarettes a day, for who knows how long. Chased by cigars, whenever he drank and gambled. Which, as I understand it, was also every day. He dropped dead suddenly at age 59, when I was only nine years old. A massive heart attack.

Were tobacco products the only cause? Of course not. Did they contribute significantly? You'll never convince me otherwise. And, yes . . . I have since read the reports. The hard data the tobacco companies had for decades, linking their products to cancer and other adverse health impacts. Their relentlessness in marketing products they knew were slowly killing people.

My apologies to anyone who may still smoke!
I'll get off that soapbox! ☺

But why get on it *here*? Remember that "Opportunity of A Lifetime" at General Foods? Something *significant* happened in November of 1985. Just *three months* after I had completed my internship there. And *three months* after they had made me that great post-graduation offer.

General Foods was acquired by Phillip Morris.
In a $5.6 billion transaction.

So, I couldn't have worked there *anyway* . . . could I, Lord? I just didn't *know* it then . . . but *You* did. And You had guided my steps . . . even though I <u>still</u> didn't know You. And that Love I mentioned? We're still going strong . . . over *thirty years later.* ☺

But what about the *next* thirty years?

Fast Forward . . .

What is it like to <u>know</u> we're living on Borrowed Time, Lord? In a way, we <u>all</u> are . . . whether we know it or not. Time "borrowed" from — *given by* — You. For whatever "season" You have determined.

None of us knows how much Time will be ours. We often don't realize — or appreciate — how precious that Time is. It's way too easy to take for granted that it will go on indefinitely.

At least, I did . . .
. . . until The Unthinkable happened.

It's amazing how staring into the face of Death can change our perspective, Lord. My husband is eleven years older than me. Yet, suddenly we both realized: The most unlikely scenario we could ever imagine — that I could die *first* — was now a Real Possibility. Hearing that "C" word — Cancer — and talking about "survival percentages" will do that for anyone.

Of course, <u>no</u> <u>one</u> gets out of here alive. ☺

And <u>no</u> <u>one</u> gets out of here without Valleys. Valleys of many kinds. They may not be Cancer or any other major Health Crisis. Or some life-altering Injury. They could be Job or Career Valleys. Marriage Valleys. Child or Grandchild Valleys. Money Valleys. Or a thousand others.

And for *most* Valleys, the only way <u>out</u> is *through.*

We certainly don't control the "cards" we are "dealt" in Life. Perhaps the best we can do is learn how to *play well* the cards we now hold. And some of our best teachers may be the "hands" we have blown in the past.

Thanks to You, Lord, I gave up regrets long ago. Because of how *You* have used *everything* that has ever happened to me. To help me become the "one-of-a-kind-special" person You have created me to be. So I can fulfill the Destiny You have set aside for me, and me alone.

A Destiny that pleases You . . .
. . . and changes this world for the better.

"For we are God's handiwork, created in Christ Jesus
to do good works, which God prepared in advance for us to do."
(Ephesians 2:10)

<u>We</u>. Not just <u>me</u>.
We . . . meaning whoever will open their heart to You.

"Everyone who calls on the name of the Lord will be saved."
(Joel 2:32)

There is <u>one</u> thing I would change, Lord. If I could. The Greatest Evil I ever committed. Because of the one it hurt the most. Yes, it was part of the fallout of the Greatest Evil ever committed against me. This reasoning might help explain it . . . but nothing can excuse it.

I can't go back and change it, though . . . can I, Lord? None of us can. We can never go back and change what has now become History. But, by Your Amazing Grace, we <u>can</u> *move forward.* We can *learn* from past screw-ups. And You can *use* them. Mightily. Miraculously. *For Good.*

Because not even the Greatest Evil we have ever committed, nor the Greatest Evil ever committed against us, can exempt us from receiving Your Love, Forgiveness, Healing and Hope.

"God demonstrates His own love for us in this:
While we were still sinners, Christ died for us."
(Romans 5:8)

"You intended to harm me, but God intended it for good
to accomplish what is now being done, the saving of many lives."
(Genesis 50:20)

And, yes . . . that's another story, too.
So *many* stories yet to tell…right, Lord? ☺

By Your Grace, I am still living out <u>my</u> Borrowed Time since the Valley of the Shadow. My three-month checkups lasted for the three years considered my highest risk of recurrence. My six-month checkups lasted another two years. As I write these words, I am gratefully celebrating five years Cancer Free.

Let me say that again: <u>Five years</u> CANCER FREE!!!
A HUGE Milestone, whenever Cancer has come to visit!

My hair came back, too. *Thank You, Lord!* It's different. Maybe even better? That's my story, and I'm sticking to it! ☺ It's certainly *grayer*. But like I said before: I've earned every one of those gray hairs. I've lived through every Valley that caused every one.

But I wasn't ever alone . . . was I, Lord?
Even when I didn't know You were there.

And because of You, I haven't just *lived* through those Valleys. I haven't just "survived" them. I have learned to <u>thrive</u> *despite* them. Even, while *in the middle* of them.

Maybe that explains the subtitle You gave me for this book. The Secrets You have taught me through Valleys of Life and Leadership are just as true for *Overcoming Life's Worst* as they are for *Savoring Life's Best*. And sometimes, The Best is <u>only</u> found smack dab in the *middle* of The Worst. Where we can encounter *You*, Lord, in ways that are just not possible *anywhere else.*

Because <u>You</u> are The Real Prize, Lord — The Treasure behind every Secret. And You want <u>all</u> of Life to be as rich as possible for us . . . don't You?

In ways that have *nothing* to do with money.

I've lived and led both ways, Lord — with and without You. Maybe "lived" is too generous a word for the many years I spent apart from You. More than half of my One-and-Only Life.

When I was wildly successful in the world's eyes (and mine), there was still an emptiness in me that nothing could fill. A hardness that nothing could soften. I was a "make it happen" kind of gal who, for a time, thought <u>I</u> was The Center of The Universe. I was wrong.

When I was mired in The Pit Beneath the Valley Floor, during the years I call my Black Period, I longed only for *peace.* Peace that I imagined came <u>only</u> with going to sleep and never waking up. Even if that "sleep" came by my own hand. Thankfully, I was wrong about that, too.

Yes, Lord . . . so many stories.
Stories that could have ended everything . . .
. . . but, instead, led to *New Beginnings.*

I know it is only by Your Grace that I am alive today, to share the stories in <u>this</u> book with whomever is reading them. Cancer of the soul is much more deadly than cancer of the body. Thankfully, there is a Fool-proof Cure for *that* cancer that doesn't involve the "C" word, Chemo.

It involves that much better "C" word: Christ.

And what You have promised Your children, Lord, makes this present Life — as awesome and beautiful as it can be — seem more like Dorothy's sepia-toned world in contrast to the multicolored Land of Oz. Because whatever is awaiting us in Heaven will be *so much more* . . .

"No eye has seen, no ear has heard,
no mind has conceived what God has prepared
for those who love Him."
(1 Corinthians 2:9)

I can hardly wait! But wait, I must. ☺
Meanwhile, what's next for *us*, Lord? For You and me?

One thing I know: Whatever it is, it must *matter*. Not only for now, but also *forever*. However long we may live on Planet Earth, it is hardly a blip on the radar screen of Eternity. But our "blip" is not insignificant. And once it's over, we live on <u>forever</u> . . . *somewhere*.

We each have a sphere of influence, unique only to us. And we each have stories — *powerful stories* — that need to be heard by those we are privileged to touch. Hopefully, stories that will help them turn to *You*, Lord.

So, *their* "Forever Somewhere" is *with* You . . .
 . . . not *apart* from You.

I am thrilled by our present Adventure, Lord . . . as You enable me to speak Life into Christian Women of Influence. Leaders who serve You in the Marketplace. Helping them draw closer to You than ever before. Where You help them *strive less* and *surrender more*. So they can *lead* <u>and</u> *live* more *powerfully*, more *passionately*, and more *purposefully* than ever before.

For such a time as this.
As the Day of Your Return draws ever closer.

And what about you, dear Reader?

<u>WHAT'S NEXT</u> . . . for *you?*

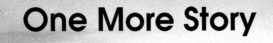

One More Story

Saving The Best for Last.

It was a desperate cry — The First Prayer of My Lifetime. When I had reached the end of my rope. Sometime in 1975 . . . when I was twenty-four years old.

"God, if You exist, then You need to help me . . .
. . . because I will not survive if You don't."

I believed He heard me . . . and slammed the door in my face. Because I was not worth His time. How could I be? I was nothing. Terminally broken.

I almost <u>did</u> die. By my own hand.
But a Revelation came. Sometime in 1977.

"You don't <u>have</u> to be a victim of what has happened to you in your life.
Some things you can't change, because they're History.
But you CAN <u>think</u> other things, and <u>feel</u> other things, and <u>do</u> other things
that are healthier for you and for the people around you."

Somehow, in that moment, I <u>knew</u> this was *True*. I had no idea back then that this Revelation was from the Lord. *But it was.* He used it to save my life . . . which did "a 180." My downhill slide became my Uphill Climb. I went from nothing to *everything*.

"Yeah, there's probably a God, but who cares? Look at ME!"

Years later, The Three Blessings happened. Each one, a Miracle. Over a period of 13 months. There's that number 13 again! ☺ I knew they were from "Him" — The God of The Universe. I just didn't know who He was.

After Blessing #1, I said The Second Prayer of My Lifetime:

"Thank You, God. I <u>know</u> this blessing is from <u>You</u>.
I don't know why You've done this.
I don't know You. I don't think about You.
I don't care about You. I'm not looking for You.
But I <u>know</u> this blessing is from <u>You</u> . . .
and I will <u>always</u> cherish it."

I meant it. And I have kept my word.

With Blessing #2, six months later, I said that same prayer — word-for-word. Out loud (just like the first time). [How was I to know God could read my thoughts? ☺]

Blessing #3 came another seven months later, through yet another Close Encounter with Death. A horrific auto accident. In the predawn darkness, it became clear I wasn't going to die. I began to say that same prayer again.

But I heard myself. *"Whoa, Diana . . . You've said this before."*
So, I *changed* the prayer:

"Maybe the best way to thank You is to learn more about You."

I was out of work for eight weeks. Bedridden for the first two, in excruciating pain. And depressed. Why was I alive? I should be dead. I wasn't some important person giving money away to great causes or doing good for others. Truth be told, Life was pretty much all about Me.

I remembered The Prayer and thought, *"How can I learn more about Him?"* His answer was immediate:

"Read the Bible."

I had no idea it was Him, of course. I thought:
"What I great idea I just had! I've never read the Bible. I'll read the Bible."

Two days later, I began physical therapy. Which became three days a week for the next nine months. I went for my first session and met the physical therapist assigned to me.

I said, *"Tell me a little bit about yourself."*

She told me her name, and . . . the <u>second</u> thing she said to me was:

"One of the things I like to do in my spare time is teach people how to read the Bible."

The hair on my neck stood up! I thought I was in an episode of that old classic, *The Twilight Zone*. Something strange — *supernatural* — was happening . . . and I was freaking out! I didn't say a word. I just went home . . . and realized:

The God of The Universe had just spoken *to me.*

*"You want to read the Bible? Here's a resource to help you.
But you know what? It's totally your choice.
If you don't say anything, she'll never know what's <u>really</u> going on here."*

I went back two days later and told her I didn't think it was a coincidence that she had been assigned to me. When she heard the story, she agreed and asked when I wanted to start. *"How about today?"* I said. *"I don't think we're supposed to wait."*

She gave me a Bible and steered me to the book of John. I began reading about Jesus. And I had to admit . . . He sounded *wonderful*. But she didn't understand. She didn't know all that had happened to me in my life, or all I had done in response.

The Victim I had been. The Victimizer I had become.

He couldn't mean all He offered
— *all He promised* — could be *mine.*

She didn't argue with me or try to convince me. She just kept saying, *"Keep reading."* So, I did. And two months later, I realized Jesus *did* mean me . . . like He means *every one of us.*

I was in my mid-thirties. I couldn't deny that He had come after me. And after reading His Words every day for two months, asking every question I could think to ask, I ran out of reasons to <u>not</u> turn my Life over to Him. So, I did just that — I turned my Life over to Him.

On May 20, 1987.

It wasn't pretty. I didn't know "right" words to say, based on any formula. I just got on my face before Him. For five hours. Speaking my heart to Him. Crying my guts out, at times. Not understanding what I was "signing up for." Just knowing I had to finally stop running.

Isn't that all You want from <u>any</u> of us, Lord?

"OK, Lord . . . I give up.
You obviously want me. You came after me.
I don't know why. <u>I'm</u> <u>not</u> <u>worth</u> <u>it</u>. But, I'm tired of running.
So, take my Life . . . and do whatever You want with it."

That's how it started . . . what has turned out to be
The <u>Greatest</u> Adventure of My Lifetime!

How about you, dear Reader?
Are *you* living this Adventure, too?

If so, *press in . . .* and *press on!* ☺

If not . . . I hope you will give Jesus a look.
A Real Look. Not a superficial glance.

Look at His Words, with an open mind. Look *deeply* . . . and you will see into His *heart.* And when you do, I hope you discover what I already *know* is true . . .

How very much He loves you, too.
Like no one else ever <u>can</u> . . . or <u>will</u>.

Isn't that worth discovering?

My Personal Invitation

Isn't it amazing — *mind-boggling,* at times —
how the Lord connects us this side of Heaven?!

How Strangers can encourage and help each other . . .
How Helpers can become Colleagues . . .
How Colleagues can become Friends . . .
How Friends can become Family . . .

. . . changing our lives — and the world — for the better . . .

. . . even if we have never met face-to-face?!

I pray this book has blessed you, dear Reader.
Some of you may want to connect with me going forward . . .
either through this work or beyond it.

With all my heart, I invite you to do so.

Here are some possible ways:

Check out my website:
www.championsofdestiny.com

Follow my blog:
www.championsofdestiny.com/blog

Use more copies of *Victory in The Valley*
to start a small group . . .
applying the 7 Secrets to your own
Leadership and Personal Valleys.

E-mail me (I would love to know how this book touched you!):
diana@championsofdestiny.com

Sign up for a Complimentary Coaching Call with me:
http://tinyurl.com/DianaFurr

Call me directly:
863-446-1660

If you are feeling a "heart prompting" to connect with me,
please don't ignore it.

If you've read this far, it probably won't surprise you when I say
I believe such promptings are Heaven-sent.

Wouldn't it be something to discover
wherever the Lord might want to lead us . . .
. . . *together?*

Appendix

My Prayer on Day 1 of Chemo
May 5, 2011

Dearest Lord: Today is the day.
I showered and prepared to go to Moffitt for
the port insertion and lab work. The infusion begins at noon.

I stood naked before You as I showered and cleansed my body with soap.
I am always naked before You, Lord. You know me inside and out.
Nothing is hidden from You. You know the thoughts and intentions
of my heart . . . the desires of my heart . . .
my hopes and dreams . . . my need for You.
I have prayed since 4:00 AM and declared all these things . . .

You are my Life and my Love . . . My Forever Father,
My Forever Husband, My Forever Soul-Lover, My Forever Friend.
Once again, I place my life and my spirit into Your hands.
I thank You for Your love and grace to me . . . for Your mercy . . .
for Your Great and Precious Promises, which sustain me.
You are the Bread of Life and I "feed" on You now
as the Best Meal I will ever consume.
Whatever Your enemies have meant for evil, You have meant for good . . .
and You have transformed it for Your good purposes and Your glory.
I pray the Blood of Jesus over the port and the chemicals
that will be inserted into my body today . . .
that they may be sanctified and set aside for Your sacred use.

I overcome the enemy by the Blood of the Lamb
and the word of my testimony.
With the authority You have given me, in the Name of Jesus,

I bind Satan and his minions and cast them
out of my life and these proceedings.
I break any curse and scheme, by the Blood of the Lamb,
and declare by Your Word that
no weapon formed against me will prosper . . .
I render them futile and powerless, by the mighty name of Jesus Christ
and His Power which has already raised me from the dead.

In the name of Jesus, I bind discouragement, disease, death, depression,
anxiety, fear, confusion, weakness, fatigue, nausea, baldness, infection
and every possible adverse side effect . . .
and I loose every fruit of the Holy Spirit (Love, Joy, Peace, Patience,
Kindness, Goodness, Faithfulness, Gentleness and Self-Control).
I loose victory, health, vibrant life, energy, appetite for nutritious food,
clarity of thinking and eternal purpose, wisdom, discernment,
strength, courage, boldness and Holy Spirit anointing.

I offer my life to You today, Lord, as a living sacrifice
— holy (by Your sacrifice) and pleasing to You (by Your grace) —
as my spiritual act of worship today.

I declare, by the Blood of Jesus,
that this chemo is a sacred instrument in Your Healing Hands,
meant only for my good . . .
rendering complete destruction of every cancer cell
that may yet be present in my body, and
releasing complete protection of every other cell from harm.
I declare Your Word, which is ALWAYS TRUE:
Jeremiah 29:11, Romans 8:28, 2 Corinthians 4, 2 Corinthians 5:17-21 . . .
and I receive these words as Your personal gift to me.

Have Your way, Lord . . . It's ALL ABOUT YOU.
And please meet my precious husband in his every need . . .
that this season will bring him eternal riches he has not even imagined!

You are with me . . . I feel You right here.

I see You in all things and I know that You are <u>good</u>,
ALL THE TIME.
As You walk with me (and carry me) today,
show me the work You have set aside for me to do . . .
and empower me, by Your Holy Spirit, to be
a blessing to all those I encounter today.

Today is the day You have made!
I rejoice and am glad in it!
Another Gift of Life!

As ever, with my love, hugs and kisses . . .

Abba's Girl

Notes

INTRODUCTION

1. The definition of "Miracle" came from Oxford Dictionaries online, downloaded on December 12, 2016: https://en.oxforddictionaries.com/definition/miracle

SECRET #4

1. Through Caring Bridge, a non-profit organization, people going through major health challenges can establish a personal website where health updates, photos and videos can be shared with people who care about them. Caring Bridge provides this service free, and encourages charitable donations to help support its efforts. Visit their website for all details: https://www.caringbridge.org/

Acknowledgement Prayers

Oh, Lord . . . How can I possibly list everyone who has helped bring this book forth, both in my life and on these pages? Certainly, there are many people — known and unknown to me — who have made a profound difference. Through their words and actions. Even, *especially*, through their prayers.

I am so grateful to know
that the blessing they have been to me
is *not* unknown to *You* . . .

. . . and that a reward far more precious than my "thanks"
awaits them in the Gift of *Your* "Well done!"

So, I gratefully pray for those acknowledged here and those who remain unnamed . . . asking You to give *all* of them a double-portion of *all* that is most precious to You. In the form of whatever *tangible* Touch they need from You . . . to assure them of Your Faithful Provision, Your Unfailing Love, and Your Very-Present Help. And whatever *intangible* Touch they need from You . . . to open the vaults of treasures too priceless to measure.

Treasures like . . .
Joy that Strengthens,
Peace that Protects,
Grace that Suffices,
Life that Redeems,
and Hope that is Unstoppable . . .
. . . no matter what.

For now, I acknowledge . . .

You, Lord . . . The Giver of Life, in all its fullness.
Now and Forever.

My husband, Bud — my treasured partner and faithful friend throughout most of my adult life. I fell "head over heels" when we met. We "signed up" for one kind of life together . . . then *You* showed up, Lord. And he kept loving me — even when You took Your rightful place in my heart. What a wrestling match that turned out to be . . . for both of us! ☺ Thank You for filling our life together with Adventure and Delight. And for helping him stick *with* me and *by* me in tougher times — even as I was learning to love *You* well, so I could learn to love *him* well . . . succeeding and failing along the way. My life is *so much richer* because of him. Bless my Buddy, Lord, in ways that are unmistakable and irresistible. I know You have . . . and I trust You *will.*

The medical team You assembled for me at Moffitt Cancer Center — Doctors Christine Laronga, Paul Smith and Susan Minton, Advanced Registered Nurse Practitioners Laurie Sullivan and Heather Roulstone, to name a few . . . and the countless others whose expertise and encouragement helped me navigate through such uncharted waters. Bless them, Lord, with divinely-inspired breakthroughs . . . and soul-renewing Joy for every life saved. Joy that strengthens their perseverance, sustaining them when any life is lost.

The Caring Bridge ministry. What an amazing platform You inspired them to create! Thank You, Lord, for using them to mobilize so much prayer and encouragement on my behalf. And for giving me a place where I could write the words You unexpectedly put in my heart . . . and, in so doing, discover the gift and passion for writing You have planted in me. Bless them with supernatural provision — a good measure, pressed down and overflowing — so that *countless* others will be blessed as I was.

The staff, volunteers and supporters at Samaritan's Touch Care Center. You decided to do something *awe-inspiring* in our lives and our community, Lord. So, You stirred *countless* people — too many to name here — to join You. Those with much and those with little gave generously of their time, talent and treasure . . . blessing *thousands*, yet receiving *far more* —

in unforgettable encounters with *You*. Bless them all with a felt sense of Your Pleasure, Lord . . . and even *greater* Protection and Provision, as the need grows and the Labor of Love continues.

My business and life coach, Pam Wolf. My beloved Forever Sister-in-Christ . . . who, like me, fell for You later in life. I am forever grateful to You, Lord, for the Gift she is to me. For how she . . . inspires me with her love and devotion to You . . . advises me with godly counsel, prayerfully-discerned . . . enlightens me, when she sees in me what I cannot see . . . fights for me, when the Adversary predictably and persistently comes against me . . . and so much more. Enlarge her territory, Lord, and bless her with a double portion of Your Spirit as You continue to anoint her to change the world for You.

My "Sistas" — Kathy ("Katt") Perry, Elle Dewyngaert, Kathy Mee, Debbie Lees, Moddie Desselle, and Diana Albritton ("The Other Diana" ☺) . . . all of them, there from the start. And Julia Hinshaw and Candace North, who came later. Sisterhood *is* powerful . . . especially in *Your* Family, Lord! I am thankful for . . . every laugh (and tear) we share . . . every joy (and burden) we celebrate (and carry) together . . . every Sista-lunch, cyber-hug and chocolate chip cookie. ☺ For how we walk together, even in darkness . . . and help each other see Your Light. They are so dear to me, Lord . . . dearer still, to You. Bless them in ways that leave no room for doubt.

The Jericho Team and our OMC family — the intercessors and pastors You assembled, Lord, as You called me out of the Valley of the Shadow. In those early post-chemo days, I didn't have strength to do much more than pray. Exactly where I needed to be, so You could teach me that Spirit-directed *prayer* — filtered through Your Love — is *the most powerful force* on Earth. You continue to stir our sense of urgency to pray for each other and the region/state/nation where You have placed us. Bless us all with Answers that will *spur us on*.

The clients I have come to love, Lord . . . and those yet to come. Christian Women of Influence, gathering in Your Presence *expectantly*. Knowing that our business or ministry, even our very leadership, is our *calling* from You — our unique opportunity to impact *our* part of the greater world for *You*. For such a time as this. Seeking Your wisdom, clarity and direction. Finding all that and something far more precious: *Intimacy* with You. Bless and empower these amazing women to whom You have entrusted so much. By Your Spirit, may the breadth and depth of their impact for You grow *exponentially*.

My publisher, David Biebel. You are "up to" something special here, Lord. Why else would You have reconnected us after more than twenty years since our first meeting? We have offered this work into Your hands, to do with as You please. And we eagerly anticipate the blessing You will make of this in the lives of many people who are desperate for Your Touch . . . ourselves, included.

With all this and more in my heart, Lord . . . I give You The Last Word. Better yet, the punctuation *after* The Last Word. May it be, for each of us, an exclamation point! Because we have experienced *Passion-igniting, Purpose-fulfilling,* and *Power-instilling* encounters with *You*. In our Valleys of many kinds . . . and beyond.

What better place could there be, Lord,
from which to live and lead?! ☺

Victory in The Valley

7 Secrets to Overcoming Life's Worst and Savoring Life's Best

STUDY GUIDE

Don't miss out on this *Great New Resource* . . .
a chapter-by-chapter *Study Guide*
to help you apply the **7 Secrets** to your own Life!

GO TO the link below to get your FREE copy!

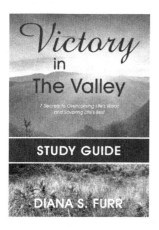

Perfect as individual devotional
and/or small group curriculum!

Thought-provoking questions +
space to record God's answers
and your spiritual insights.

Downloadable companion to
Victory in The Valley –
*7 Secrets to Overcoming Life's Worst
and Savoring Life's Best*

Your personal "Travel Log" and "Treasure Map" as you . . .
. . . "flashback" to your *own* Valleys-past, and
. . . "fast forward" to your *own* Valleys-present . . .
. . . so you can *discover* and *embrace* your *own*
Life-transforming *Victory in The Valley!*

This downloadable PDF is available exclusively from
Author Diana S. Furr at her website:

www.ChampionsofDestiny.com/victory-in-the-valley
Click: FREE Study Guide

Diana S. Furr, Founder – Champions of Destiny, LLC
Send your questions and comments to: diana@championsofdestiny.com

CPSIA information can be obtained
at www.ICGtesting.com
Printed in the USA
LVOW01s2347250417

532120LV00022B/591/P